EATING OUT

IN

PROVENCE

AND THE

COTE D'AZUR

ACKNOWLEDGEMENTS

First I want to thank Dan Air for sponsoring my programme on Riviera Radio for the last few years. This has certainly given me much of the material for the area of Les Alpes Maritimes in this book. I have also enjoyed many pleasant trips on their airline, thanks to the smiling welcome of their staff and their excellent care. There are also all those at Riviera Radio, especially my presenters Lucienne Joy and Daevid Fortune, who deserve my thanks.

I want to thank all those friends and colleagues who invited me to their favourite restaurant; without these this guide would have been very slim. Also those who accompanied me on some of those long journeys, especially where we were disappointed with the meal. To those listeners who also directed me to some great places; to some of the restaurant owners who imparted some special history of their place or region, or opened my eyes to some of their new dishes, my special thanks. I must point out that those restaurants are very hard working, generally busy six days a week; they start early, buying produce, then preparing dishes for that day, trying out and costing new recipes. All these tasks take time. Complain if anything is poor, either food or service, but forgive them if they occasionally have a bad day.

EATING OUT

IN

PROVENCE

AND THE

COTE D'AZUR

EDWARD ROCH

INTERLINK BOOKS
NEW YORK

DEDICATION

I dedicate this book to my wonderful wife Sandie and children Carla, Victoria and Andrew, who suffered much, travelling miles, and trying out new places, some, certainly, not good enough to mention in this book. They have also borne with me as I gained 12 kilos (26 pounds). Now they are putting up with my short temper as I try to lose those ugly additions – the next book will certainly be about losing weight and still eating out. I must also remember my parents who brought me up appreciating all the good things in life, especially good food.

First American edition published 1992 by

INTERLINK BOOKS

An imprint of Interlink Publishing Group, Inc.
99 Seventh Avenue, Brooklyn, New York 11215

Published simultaneously in Great Britain by Rosendale Press, Ltd

Library of Congress Cataloging-in-Publication Data

Roch, Edward.
    Eating out in Provence and the Côte d'Azur / Edward Roch. — 1st American ed.
        p.   cm.
    Includes index.
    ISBN 0-940793-93-8 (pb)
    1. Restaurants, lunch rooms, etc.—France—Provence—Guidebooks.
2. Provence (France)—Guidebooks.   I. Title.
    TX907.5.F72P767   1992
    647.95444'9—dc20

92-4803
CIP

Cover design by Robert Budwig
Maps by Alistair Powell

Printed in Italy by G. Canale & C. S.p.A. - Borgaro T.se - TURIN

ISBN 0-940793-93-8

CONTENTS

INTRODUCTION

This guide has been written because many of my listeners to Radio Riviera wanted to expand their knowledge of restaurants offering good value in their area. It is also written to help those who are travelling from the north to find places where they can enjoy good eating from the moment they enter Provence. I hope they will also find it helpful that I have given a brief description of many of the towns and villages where the recommended restaurants are found. This description includes some historical notes and places of interest that might be visited.

In the opening section there are some useful hints, including translations of the names of fish. The first time I saw *brochet* on the menu I automatically presumed it was a mass of items skewered and grilled. What a surprise when a piece of pike was served in front of me. You will also find a list of Provençal wines, Provençal cheeses and the ten smelliest cheeses in France and a description of the ways of finding the great truffle. All these hints will help you enjoy this wonderful area.

Most of the places were first visited on the recommendation of local friends or one of my listeners. Many more were visited than listed, as some were very disappointing and others much too expensive. This area of France, due to the demands of the visiting French and other nationalities, offers excellent food but prices have run away with themselves, so for this reason it is important to choose carefully where to eat.

I have generally eaten in the places recommended in this guide, with a friend or a member of my family. Frequently there have been more than two of us. The descriptions are honest, yet I know sometimes if you are with an amusing group or the place itself is in festive mood, the restaurant critic can become biased. Luckily many of the places have also been visited by my listeners after they have heard my programme and they certainly would have complained on the open line. Some of the most interesting restaurants are those where I have stopped simply because the car park was full with local licence plated cars (the latter are, of course, much easier to spot in mainland Europe).

This guide starts in north-west Provence and works southwards and eastwards so ending on the Côte d'Azur. The restaurants are listed under the town where they are situated and have their owners' names, addresses and telephone numbers. It always pays to book and if you decide not to go please, out of politeness, telephone to cancel. Remember lunch starts at noon in Provence; most shops and businesses close until two o'clock. It may be difficult to find places after 12.30pm, so please book. After 1.30pm some places stop serving. Occasionally you will find an address missing; this is due to the establishment being in a tiny village or very well known. 'La Meranda', in Nice, doesn't have a telephone, so in this case you have to get there early. In the towns where I recommend a restaurant, I also list the very famous eating places nearby that are in all the well-known French gastronomy guides, to be generally helpful, although these temples of gastronomy are not what this guide is about.

When I visit a restaurant I don't let them know I am a food critic with a programme on Monte Carlo's Radio Riviera (FM 106.5). I try to write down without being seen as much as possible. Having talked with the server or proprietor and after listening to his or her recommendations I then order. I generally stick to the fixed price menu. The *menu du jour* or *du marché* are the ones that offer the food that has been purchased for that day. When I have paid the bill and I feel it is a place I will speak about I usually give the owner my card and say I will telephone him to tell him the date we will be discussing his particular restaurant on the air. It is an open-line programme so people can ring in and comment or offer advice. I also receive letters from many listeners who wish to remain anonymous.

Introduction

Since the owners are listed, when you telephone to book I would advise you to ask for them by name. This will give the impression that you know the place. They will then generally give you a better table. When you arrive ask for the owner, but check the guide because sometimes the owner is the chef so he won't be free to lead you to the table. In many cases it is a family affair, so it will be Madame who runs the restaurant.

A last word of advice in my introduction: if you find anything that doesn't reach the quality you expect, or you are disappointed with the service, please ask to speak to the owner and complain. I am sure you will find they will rectify the fault, but please do not wait till the meal is over. Don't simply say to yourself: 'I am not coming back here again'. Standards are high in France because the general population expect to be well served and well fed if they are paying for it. I must say when a French person complains the owner certainly listens. We must do likewise at home and abroad.

If you are a gourmet or you just enjoy good food, France is the place for you. Some of us are lucky to live here. There is a whole spectrum of restaurants. France is the country that sets the standard and every other country, whether it likes it or not, is measured against it. Why has France achieved this reputation for good food and good service? My feeling is that it comes first from the French household, and this has continually improved in standard. France's Sun King Louis XIV ate in public every day. People saw what he was served and wanted the same when they returned home. Other reasons include the wide range of climatic differences, from the north where they were used to heavier dishes, to the south where they were accustomed to a wide variety of salads and vegetables that grew all year round. Then there were the different trees and plants brought in by centuries of invaders. The Greeks imported olive trees and vines, the Romans brought in a variety of vegetables, flavours and aromas, the Saracens had a knowledge of spices and hardier vegetables like chick peas. The Spanish brought oranges; pasta arrived with the Holy Roman Empire. With all these the French then organised an educational training in cooking and service. This is maintained throughout France. and it is not only theoretical, but practical as well. You will find young students doing a stint in small hotels and restaurants of all standards during their vacations. If they do not do the practical they will not move up into the next year or get a qualification.

A final reason for continual improvement is to be found in French gastronomic guide books. An establishment knows that if it gains a higher grade it can charge more and discriminating customers are brought to the door by people reading these well-established guides. The oldest and leader of these is certainly the famous red *Guide Michelin*. Their ratings include the quality of the surroundings, tableware, kitchens and quality of food. Their 'star' ratings (sometimes known as 'macaroons' to French chefs) are hard to win yet more and more restaurants have been awarded them. The *Gault Millau* guide has more extensive and personal descriptions of the place and the dishes and the authors give marks out of twenty. They offer *toques* for the mighty. There are also the *Bottin Gourmand*, that works *département* by *département* and the *Relais Chateaux*, *Logis de France* and the *Routier*; all guides of considerable influence on where to stay and where to eat.

All of these guides must maintain their standard of rating of establishments. The restaurants must fight to improve their standard, otherwise they will be dropped because there are always other places trying to be rated.

This guide fills a gap since no other guide judges restaurants mainly on good value for money. We also generally describe a total meal, the service and ambiance and then rate the restautant out of ten.

A great number of people think it is simple to discover a special restaurant. One, yes: a large number is difficult and without help and careful observasion it is certainly not easy. Many people want to take friends to that special find that no one else knows. Hopefully you will find that some of these recommended restaurants are exactly that. *Bon appétit.*

The main points to remember are: (a) book to get a good table; (b) remember lunch is from 12 noon to 1.30pm; (c) dinner is from 7.30pm to 10.00pm; (d) tariffs for food are posted outside restaurants and for drinks are posted in bars or cafes; (e) service is included except where it is stated otherwise; (f) if you experience poor quality food or service, please call over the *patron* or manager and tell him firmly yet politely.

PROVENCE

The people of Provence were originally Ligurians, descended from Neolithic man. At the time of the Greek Empire, Marseille (Massalia) was founded as a trading post in about the seventh century BC. The colonising of Nice (Nikaia meaning Victory) and Antibes (Antipolis) happened about three centuries later. During this time the locals also mixed with the Celts from further north. Marseille is France's oldest city. The finds of Neolithic man are abundant, maybe not as old as those found in the Dordogne region, but still very early.

The perimeters of Provence were originally prescribed by the Romans, who conquered and colonised the area at the start of the first century after Christ. The name given to this area was Provincia, implying the adjacent country. The Romans treated this land over the Alps very much as we treat the provinces outside our cities. The boundaries at that time were easily defined by the Alps in the east, the sea in the south, the River Rhône in the west and the Dauphiné mountains in the north.

Both the Greeks and Romans left many wonderful historical remains, so your travels in western Provence can be a view of the past. There are fabulous remains in many towns: the theatre in Orange, the arena in Arles, the aqueduct near Nîmes. These are just some of what the different occupations left in this area. The list of foreign powers is impressive – it is the history of Europe. The Ligurians, Greeks, Romans, Visigoths, Saracens, the Popes, the House of Orange, lastly the English who were there until 1793 when Napoleon eventually got us out of Toulon. Eastern Provence has less of historical interest, but it is in even higher demand as the place to holiday and live since it offers even more facilities for sport and pleasure. This area is now better known as the Côte d'Azur.

COTE D'AZUR

This part of France is still recognised as being in Provence. The Mediterranean coast was given this name early in the nineteenth century when it was used to tempt people in the cold north to winter in the south. It became popular with the English as early as the mid-eighteenth century. Many English families lived in Nice because of its good climate and because the Dukes of Savoy and Kings of Sardinia were British allies in the maritime rivalry with France. Remember, Nice belonged to the House of Savoy until 1860.

Tobias Smollett wrote his *Travels* after a visit to Nice to recuperate from poor health. Published in the third quarter of the eighteenth century, it promoted the area and influenced many people to make the long journey for health and holiday. The arrival of the railways really accelerated this trend. The Côte d'Azur covered the area from Menton to just west of Cannes.

France generally has a huge number of restaurants. Those in the towns and country are nearly always family affairs. In many cases you can find that the same family has served the area over several generations. This type of restaurant is much harder to find in Provence, especially on the Côte d'Azur, because this part of France has experienced a population explosion, an invasion by people from the cold north and foreigners coming to settle. You will find restaurants here run by other nationalities. As the south of France is such a magnet this has created a greater demand than supply, and people with no qualification in this particular field decide it is easier to open a restaurant than go into some other *métier*.

Another variation can be noticed the further east you travel: price. It gets more expensive to eat and drink once you are on the Côte d'Azur. The local wine that you will find available for under 50 francs in a restaurant in Aix-en-Provence has doubled in price by the time you arrive near Nice. Before you enter any place for some refreshment or sustenance, look at the menu and/or drinks tariff. It has to be posted outside by law. At least you will be prepared before you enter.

Small and medium sized resort towns are less competitive in price than, for instance, Marseille or Nice. These cities have a large population who live and work there, so they have to have places to cater for them. Look for these as the food will be more attractively priced, even though they will still be more expensive than a similar establishment in Paris or Lyon.

The city that impresses me most with its choice of good value restaurants is certainly Aix-en-Provence, the old capital of Provence and a university centre. Here, in the *zone piéton* just off the Cour Mirabeau, which is the main thoroughfare, you will find an abundance of choice at great value. 'Why?' I ask every time I visit the town. They tell me it is because there is a large student population. There is also a large tourist influx. The city of Nice has similar reasons but it is still more expensive than Aix.

Standards of quality and service have risen in Provence and the Côte d'Azur during the past ten years. So you will not be surprised to hear that Mougins, near Cannes, has more restaurants rated with stars than any other small town in France. The hotels have also revamped their restaurants and employ highly qualified chefs. This means that most first class hotels now have highly rated restaurants. Certainly these very super establishments are pricey, yet for special occasions they are well worth the visit. You will find them listed in this guide.

DISCOVERING PROVENCE

This guide is written in the manner I would prefer you to discover Provence. That is, coming down from the north. If you fly to Nice or Marseille you are thrown headlong into the bustle of Provence. From the west you enter via the Camargue, a marshland that is attractive in its own way but lacks the flavour of Provence. From the east the area is very built up, and you hit the Côte d'Azur full frontal. This is the area where I live, yet sadly it is no longer as beautiful as it once was. Forest fires have denuded the hillsides of their thick carpet of greenery and this has been replaced by unsightly buildings.

The two main routes from the north are heading south from Grenoble and south from Lyon along the Rhône Valley. If you choose the former you leave the Dauphiné region and enter via the town of Sisteron. This is the famous *route Napoléon*; the road he took north on his way to the showdown at Waterloo. The area is well known for it lamb and lavender. Here Provence is at your feet. The Romans found this a hardy area yet very easy to defend as there is only a narrow entrance from the north.

The second route from Lyon via the Rhône valley is the more traditional for the past and present holiday maker. Visitors first came down the river by boat, then the railway was built and even more ventured forth. Early this century the motor car appeared and the route National 7 was built. Hordes now jostle and race down the *autoroute* in search of fun and sun. Gratefully many head westwards at Avignon, yet they have already sensed the change.

Once Lyon is behind you and you are heading towards Orange you suddenly feel this change whatever the season of the year. One senses the change in the air, it is fuller, and yes, yes it could be warmer. The atmosphere is also different. You automatically feel you are on holiday, even if you are travelling south to your work. It is in the air, in the vista, in the smell and in the feel. Difficult to describe yet your senses get the message. The pace is slower, the fields are browner, the buildings shades of orange and beige. The villages give the impression they have been unchanged for a thousand years, and some indeed have not changed in a very long time.

This is Provence. It can best be experienced in the hillside villages. Provence past and present, narrow streets, buildings weathered by the wind and sun, people content. You will find some lovely little village restaurants in these surroundings. But scenery in Provence can also be very variable; there are lavender fields in the north, the Alps in the east with many ski resorts, beaches in the south justly famous, the marshes of the Camargue with their pink flamingoes and white horses, the stony wastelands of the Crau, vineyards wherever you look, olive trees, orange and lemon trees in the streets. So different yet so abundant, but always welcoming.

Introduction

This area has been the crossroads for so many different nationalities and this has, over the centuries, created a very imaginative kitchen. Nowhere else in the world has such a diversified choice of dishes to offer. This is partly due to the fact that nowhere else had such a choice of produce. The people of Provence have used everything, truffles from the roots of oak trees, *mesclun* and other growths for salads. The flower of the courgette was thrown away everywhere else. Provence has the good fortune to be blessed with a superb climate. In the valley of the river Var on the edge of Nice they have four harvests per year. Invaders brought with them a choice of their own produce, the most valuable having been the olive tree and the vine. There was always fresh fish in plentiful supply, yet oil was also traded for dried salted fish from the north. This was because the northerners had nothing else that would travel and keep.

People are amused that not only is this region popular for people on holiday, but for those who retire. It is in fact the earliest known place that people from abroad have come to specially for retirement. I certainly do not mean in the 17th century. Orange was colonised as a retirement town for veterans of the Roman second legion at the end of the first century. Now there is also a shift towards turning this into an area to come and work. The town of Sopia Antipolis is one of the largest technical parks in Europe. Where are we going to fit everyone in?

French Names of Fish and Shell Fish Translated into English

This list of seafood in French and English is designed to help you read the menu and order the fish you really want. I know it can be a problem. As I have mentioned, I ordered a *brochet* thinking it was meat on a skewer and got pike. I was truly disappointed even though the pike turned out to be delicious. My taste buds were all prepared for meat. You will also note that sometimes the same fish has more than one name in French.

Fish

Alose	Alose or Shad
Anchois	Anchovy
Anguille	Eel
Bar	Sea bass
Barbue	Brill
Brème	Bream
Brochet	Pike
Cabillaud	Fresh cod
Carpe	Carp
Carrelet	Plaice
Chipirones	Small squid
Colin	Hake
Congre	Conger eel
Dorade or *Davrade*	Sea bream
Estocaficada	Stockfish (dried & salted)
Flétan	Halibut
Friture	Small fried fish (Whitebait)
Gardon	Small roach
Lieu	Pollack
Limande	Dab
Lotte de mer	Monkfish
Loup de mer	Sea bass
Maquereau	Mackerel
Merlan	Whiting
Morue	Salted cod
Mulet	Grey mullet
Ombre	Crayling
Perche	Perch
Pageau	Small sea bream
Plie	Plaice
Poulpe	Octopus
Raie	Skate
Rouget	Red mullet
Saint-Pierre	John Dory
Sandre	Pike perch

Sardine	Sardine
Sole	Sole
Saumon	Salmon
Tanche	Tench
Thon	Tuna
Truite	Trout
Turbot	Turbot

Shell Fish

Araignée de mer	Spider crab
Bigorneaux	Winkles
Bouquets	Prawns
Coquilles Saint-Jacques	Scallops
Crabe	Crab
Crevettes	Shrimps
Ecrevisse	Fresh water crayfish
Gambas	King prawns
Huîtres	Oysters
belons	"
fines de claire	"
marennes	"
portugaises	"
Homard	Lobster
Langouste	Spiny lobster
Langoustines	Sea crayfish
Moules	Mussels
Oursins	Sea urchins
Palourdes	Clams
Praires	Type of cockles
Tourteau	Large crab

Eggs

Most Anglo-Saxons miss their eggs when they go on holiday, thinking things are different abroad. In fact, France offers the same choice as there is elsewhere. It is harder to ask for what you want as their terminology is slightly different. I will try to explain what you need to order in French, and what is the equivalent in English.

An egg boiled for three minutes is known as *un oeuf à la coq*. This can be served with bread 'soldiers' if you ask for *avec mouillette*.

A hard boiled egg is simply *un oeuf dur*.

A scrambled egg is *un oeuf brouillé*.

A fried egg is *un oeuf au plat*.

Poached is simplest of all: *un oeuf poché*.

I don't have to give you the French for omelette – that is the French word.

Now three other French ways of doing eggs:

En gelée means a poached egg placed in the fridge to get really cold then served dressed with jelly and garnished with, perhaps, vegetables.

Mollet is a boiled egg with a soft yoke yet the white hard. Then it is put under cold water, shelled and served on hot spinach.

En cocotte is an egg removed from its shell placed in a china or earthenware container with a little butter and cream and placed in boiling water till the white of the egg just sets.

Cheeses

France is said to have 365 different cheeses, one for every day of the year. I don't know if this is actually correct, but I do know they have a vast quantity to choose from. I thought of listing them all but decided this was ridiculous. I did think you might be interested in knowing the local Provençal cheeses and the ten smelliest ones and the region they come from. Some you might already know but do try the others.

Cheeses of Provence

Cheeses produced in Provence are generally those of milk from goats (*chèvres*) and ewes (*brebis*). There is little produced from cows (*vaches*) due to the lack of sufficient good grazing land. The main cheeses fall into a few categories, yet each has a large variety due to the great number of small producers. Therefore the same cheese can vary from village to village.

In the past, to keep the cheeses edible throughout the winter months, the cheese makers marinated them in *eau-de-vie* or olive oil. Others were wrapped in leaves, especially chestnut, or covered in peppers or herbs. In fact all these protective methods gave the cheeses a different taste, flavour and smell.

The well-known cheeses are:

Brousse de la Vesouble (also known as Chèvre de Brebis)

Banon

Petit chèvre de Montagne

Picodon de Valréas

Tome de chèvre

Tomme Arlésienne

Tomme de Sospel

Tomme de Valdeblore

Tomme de Valberg

A brousse is generally a cheese from sheep's milk. It is produced by diluting the whole milk with the whey of the day before's milking. This is then heated to nearly boiling and allowed to cool and drain for three to four days. At this stage one ends up with a cheese that is white, very creamy, tender and soft but not runny, with a slight sheep smell. It can be served sweetened or with fruit. To preserve, it has to be salted and left to mature. The length of time taken depends on taste. The words *brousse* and *caille* come from the basket moulds that are used to drain the cheese.

Banon is the name of a village where certain cheeses originate. One of their specialities is a sheep's cheese wrapped in chestnut leaves, dipped in *eau-de-vie* and then left to mature. The village of Banon is on the D950 not far from Sisteron.

Petits chèvres are the small roundels of goat's cheese. These are produced by allowing the water to drain off after setting. The longer one leaves them to dry the stronger and sharper the flavour becomes.

Picodon de Valréas is the curd of goat's milk which is cooled and given a starter and kid's rennet. When it fixes, it is salted on

Eating Out in Provence

one side and hours later turned and salted on the other. Usually it takes about twelve days before it is sold.

Tome is the name given by goat-herders to small roundels of goat's cheese.

Tomme, on the other hand, is the name given by cheese makers, using any milk, for their largest pressed cheese.

The best places to buy cheeses in Provence are:

Aix-en-Provence
Gerard Paul   9 rue des Marseillais   tel: 42 23 16 84
Antibes
L'Etable   1 rue Sade   tel: 93 34 51 42
Apt
Saturday market
Arles
Wednesday market
Avignon
Fromagerie Rane   50 rue Bonneterie   tel: 90 82 63 21
Banon
Tuesday Market   Main producer: Monsieur Ripert
Beaulieu
Beau-Lieu fromage   6 ave Maréchal Foch   tel: 93 01 05 51
Brignoles
Saturday market
Cagnes-sur-Mer
La Fermière   10 rue Giacosa   tel: 93 20 67 69
Cannes
Ceneri et fils   22 rue Meynadier   tel: 93 39 63 68
Crèmerie royale   114 rue d'Antibes   tel: 93 38 53 66
Carpentras
Friday market
Digne
Saturday market
Draguignan
Wednesday and Saturday markets
Forcalquier
Monday market

Gap
Saturday market
Grasse
Fromagerie Thouron 4 rue Thouron   tel: 93 36 56 91
Marseille
Fromagerie des Alpes 18 rue Fontange   tel: 91 47 06 23
Monaco
Arsena   1 rue Saige   tel: 93 30 99 68
Maccagno et fils   7 bis rue Acores   tel: 93 30 31 12
Nice
Tuesday market
Ferme Fromagère   27 rue Lepante   tel: 93 62 52 34
Edelweiss Fromager 55 rue France   tel: 93 87 00 12
Orange
Thursday market
Roquebrune-Cap-Martin
La Bergerie   183 avenue A Briand tel: 93 35 88 22
Saint Maximin
Friday market
Salon
Gerard Paul   35 bvd Clemenceau   tel: 90 56 29 41
Sospel
Thursday market
Vence
Friday market

Ten smelliest cheeses in France and their regions

1.	Epoisses	Burgundy
2.	Munster	Alsace and Vosges
3.	Maroilles	Flanders
4.	Livarot	Normandy
5.	Boulette d'Avesnes	Flanders
6.	Camembert	Normandy
7.	Langres	Champagne
8.	Chaumes	Dordogne
9.	Dauphin	Flanders
10	Carré de l'est	Champagne and Lorraine

Wines of Provence

There have been wines in Provence for well over two thousand years. The Greeks first brought vines with them in 600 BC, but it was the Romans who really expanded the wine production during their four hundred years of occupation. This century has seen another great surge of planting, with the growth in demand for French wine, especially in the sweep from Châteauneuf-du-Pape near Avignon through Coteaux d'Aix around Aix-en-Provence on to Côtes de Provence, now a vast *appellation* stretching along the Mediterranean coast east of Toulon almost to Cannes and north-wards beyond Draguignan. Each is home to scores of vineyards, so that you will encounter a veritable roll-call of local Châteaux and Domaines on many wine lists in the region.

Although it used to be a cliché that in Provence you drink only rosé and some rough red wines, nowadays you will find a great variety of good local wines, often at quite reasonable prices (especially if you visit the vineyards to buy direct), and a handful of really fine ones. For instance, the tiny *appellation* of Palette, with just two châteaux close to Aix, produces wonderful reds.

The approval or accreditation of wine in France is under the control of the Institut National des Appellations d'Origine (INAO). The INAO sets standards everything, from how the vines should be grown to the amount of wine that can be produced per hectare. The Institut has three basic grades. When you purchase your wine this is one of the definitions to look for, the others being the name of the producer and the year of growth.

The three grades, in order of quality, are:

AC or AOC

This stands for *'Appellation Contrôlée'* or *'Appellation d'Origine Contrôlée'* which guarantees that the wine comes from a particular region or community. This is only a partial guarantee of quality, but it does guarantee the origin, the production method and the quantity of grape variety. There is also a set quantity of litres per hectare

VDQS

This stands for *'Vin Délimité de Qualité Supérieure'*, the next category down. A great number of very old and good VDQS have now been upgraded to AC. This grade can produce more wine per hectare than AOC.

Vin de Pays

This simple local wine still has the same controls, but can produce more wine per hectare than VDQS. It is still made to a standard.

There are many *appellations* in Provence, some very large like 'Côtes de Provence', and others well known like 'Châteauneuf-du-Pape'. With each area the wines vary in taste according to the types of grape and the make-up of the ground the vines are grown in. The south facing hills usually produce higher alcohol levels, due to the sun being the catalyst in making the grape sweeter.

I am going to describe the different wine areas of Provence by following the same route we will take with the restaurants. And in each area I list some good, inexpensive wines, followed by the well-known ones. The prices are those at the vineyard itself.

Côtes du Rhône-Villages

To begin with, the broad *appellation* for much of the wine made along the Rhône valley between Vienne and Avignon is Côtes du Rhône-Villages which embraces villages such as Cairanne and Valréas near Orange, where our restaurant tour commences. It includes, too, Beaumes-de-Venise which besides producing pleasant reds and rosés, under the Côtes du Rhône-Villages *appellation*, has its own AOC for its well-known sweet white dessert wines from the Muscat grape, which must contain at least 110 grams of sugar. Several other nearby communities, such as Gigondas and Vacqueyras, making fruity red wines, rate their own *appellation*.

Côtes du Rhône-Villages

Caves des Vignerons de Rasteau	Red	White	Rosé	F20–30
Cave des Coteaux de Cairanne	Red	White	Rosé	F30–50
Domaine Sainte-Anne,				
Saint-Gervais	Red	White		F30–70

Beaumes-de-Venise

Cave des Vignerons de Beaumes-de-Venise	Muscat white	F30–50
Domaine de Durban	Muscat white	F50–70

Gigondas

Château de Montmirail	Red	F30–50

Vacqueyres

Domaine le Sang des Cailloux	Red	F30–50

Châteauneuf-du-Pape

This area of vineyards originates from the time the Popes were in Avignon, during the XIVth century. The new appellation dates only from 1923 when Baron Le Roy laid down the strict rules for the production of wine in this area. In fact these controls were the foundation for all the present French *appellations*.

The Châteauneuf *appellation* is the largest, volume wise, in the Rhône valley. There are thirteen different grapes in the make up of the wine, the main one being *grenache* and then there are *syrah* and *mourvèdre*, in lesser proportions.

The main wine is a dark and strong red with a dusty taste. White and rosé are also produced, but these are not as well known.

Le Cellier des Princes	Red	White	Rosé	F30–50
Château du Bois de la Garde	Red			F20–30
Château de Vallonnière	Red	White		F20–30
Clos des Papes	Red	White		under F80
(Quite a number of top class restaurants stock this wine.)				
Château Fortia	Red	White		under F80
Château de la Gardine	Red	White		F100
Château de Beaucastel	Red	White		F40–150

Côtes du Ventoux

This is one of the younger *appellations*, for wines grown on the southern slopes of Mont Ventoux. Quite a number of the vineyards belong to large producers from the Rhône Valley, including Château de Beaucastel and others from Beaumes-de-Venise and

Châteauneuf-du-Pape. Here the vineyards are on slopes at higher altitudes, so while the grapes at Châteauneuf remain warm at night, here they tend to get very cold. This means the *vendange* is later and the alcohol content lower.

For red wines the region tends to use *carignan, cuisault, syrah, mourvèdre,* and *grenache.* For white it is the *clairette* grape. The wines are produced in large quantities, as the vineyards are large, and not kept for very long, so they are generally sold inexpensively. They are still made to a good standard, but they are not wines that have been aged in wooden casks and are not worth laying down.

Cave de Canteperdix	Red	White	Rosé	F10–20

Their Vin du Pays is sold at well under F10.

Domaine de Champ-Long		White	Rosé	F20–30
Cave Les Roches Blanches	Red	White	Rosé	F20–30
Château Talaud	Red			F20–30
Dom. des Anges	Red	White		F25–40

Côtes du Luberon

This region, which won its AOC in 1988, grows predominantly the *carignan* grape, for red wines, but now it is being superseded by the *grenache, syrah, mourvèdre,* and *cabernet-sauvignon.* The white is produced more and more from the *chardonnay* grape, and the *cuisault* is used for the rosé. The wines were originally grown as a *vin de table,* so they still can be bought relatively cheaply.

Cave de Bonnieux	Red	White	Rosé	F10–20
Château la Sable	Red	White	Rosé	F20–30
Château Val Joanis	Red	White	Rosé	F20–30
Château de Mille	Red	White	Rosé	F30–60

(This has been a vineyard since the XIIIth century and it was also the home of one of the Popes.)

Château la Canorgue	Red	White	Rosé	F30–50

Coteaux-d'Aix-en-Provence

This *appellation* spreads through the *département* of Bouches-du-Rhône and east into the Var. While many of the best vineyards are within twenty or thirty kilometres of Aix-en-Provence, there is also a sub-division to the west, often known as Coteaux des Baux, close to the village of Les Baux with its cluster of well-known restaurants. The wine lists there tend to feature these Coteaux des Baux vineyards.

This region grew vines before any other in France and it remains one of the largest wine-growing areas, with over 100,000 acres planted. Red, rosé and white wines are produced in abundance. The red comes mainly from the *grenache* grape, aided by the *mourvèdre, syrah, counoise* and *cabernet-sauvignon* varieties. The rosés originate with *cabernet, grenache* and *syrah* vines. In recent years there has been a trend to produce more white wines, despite the strong Provençal sun, from *clairette, ugni* and *grenache blanc* grapes. This has not always been successful, although vineyards such as Château Bas and Domaine de la Cremade produce pleasing whites. But the region is best known for its reds and rosés, which may often be bought at very acceptable prices below 30 francs.

Château Barbelle	Red White	Rosé	F20–30
Château de Fonscolombe	Red White	Rosé	F20–50
Château de Calisanne	Red White	Rosé	F30–50
Château Revelette	Red White	Rosé	F20–30
Château La Coste	Red White	Rosé	F20–30
(I order this regularly when I am in this region.)			
Château de Beaupré	Red White	Rosé	F30–50
Château Vignelaure	Red	Rosé	F40–60
Mas Sainte Berthe	Red	Rosé	F30–50
(Coteaux des Baux)			

Palette

This tiny *appellation* by the *autoroute* A 8 as you head east from Aix-en-Provence produces a memorable red wine with just a tang of Provençal herbs and pines. But besides being spicy, it is pricey. At Château Simone, the main producer, the red and white cost 100 to 150 francs a bottle; rather more than that on restaurant wine lists.

Coteaux Varois

This region, which you pass through on the A 8 *autoroute* near the towns of St-Maximin-la-Ste-Baume and Brignoles, does not yet rate a full *appellation controlée*, but is the next step down, a VDQS. The vineyards, sandwiched between Coteaux d'Aix and Côtes de Provence, produce an unpretentious selection of red, rosé and white wines that can be bought cheaply at the vineyards and are often good value on the wine lists of the local restaurants you will find in the guide.

Abbaye de Saint-Hilaire	Red			under F30
Dom. des Annibale	Red		Rosé	under F30
Dom. du Loou	Red	White		under F30

Bandol

Down by the Mediterranean, just before you reach Toulon, is Bandol with terraced vineyards, planted principally with the *mourvèdre* grape, producing a rich, soft red wine. There is some rosé and white made too, but go for the reds, even though their prices are climbing a bit.

Château de Castillon	Red	White	Rosé	F30–50
Domaine de Frégate	Red		Rosé	F30–50
Domaine de la Tour du Bon	Red			F30–30
Château Sainte-Anne	Red			F50–70
Domaine Tempier	Red			F70 up

Cassis

Cassis, just along the rocky coast from Bandol, dates its first precise reference to a vineyard from 1199. Its reputation stands on its white wines based on the *ugni* grape, which go so well with the seafood in the little restaurants around the harbour.

Domaine du Paternel	White	F30–50
Château de Fontblanche	White	F30–50
Domaine de la Ferme Blanche	White	F30–50
Clos Val Bruyère	White	F50–70

Côtes-de-Provence

This *appellation* spans a wide range of vineyards mainly in Var, but with a few vineyards extending into Bouches-du-Rhône and Alpes-Maritimes. More than half the production is still of rosé, produced primarily for tourists, but in recent years there has been a determined effort to improve the output and quality of red for the local French. Many more *grenache* vines have been planted, at the expense of *carignan* which used to predominate.

The sheer diversity of the region in climate and terrain makes for great diversity in wines. Personally I find that the expensive wines are often not much better than many inexpensive ones. I would class, for example, Château Minuty, Château Ste-Rosaline and Domaine Ott on a par, yet their prices vary enormously. This is merely due to marketing. The best wine in the region that I have tasted comes from a vineyard of under five acres north of Nice called Le Clos Saint Joseph. This wonderful wine is produced by Antoine Sassi, who inherited the vineyard from his in-laws and changed it into something special. Most of his wines go to the best restaurants on the Côte d'Azur.

Dom. des Bormettes	Red	White	Rosé	F15–20
Château du Puget	Red	White	Rosé	F15–25
Château Maravenne	Red		Rosé	F20–30
Château du Galoupet	Red	White		F20–30
Château de Rasque	Red	White	Rosé	F30–70
Dom. de Launes	Red			F20–30
Dom. de la Jeannette			Rosé	F20–30
Dom. de l'Aumerade			Rosé	F50–70
Château Ferry Lacombe	Red	White	Rosé	F50–70
Commanderie de Peyrassol	Red	White	Rosé	F20–40
Château de Roux	Red	White	Rosé	F30–45
Château de St Julien d'Aille	Red		Rosé	F25–45
Château Minuty	Red	White	Rosé	F50–70
Château Barbeyrolles	Red	White	Rosé	F35–55
Château Ste Rosaline	Red	White	Rosé	F40–65
Dom. de la Bernarde	Red	White	Rosé	F50–70
Le Clos St Joseph	Red	White	Rosé	F60–70
Domaine Ott		White	Rosé	F70–90

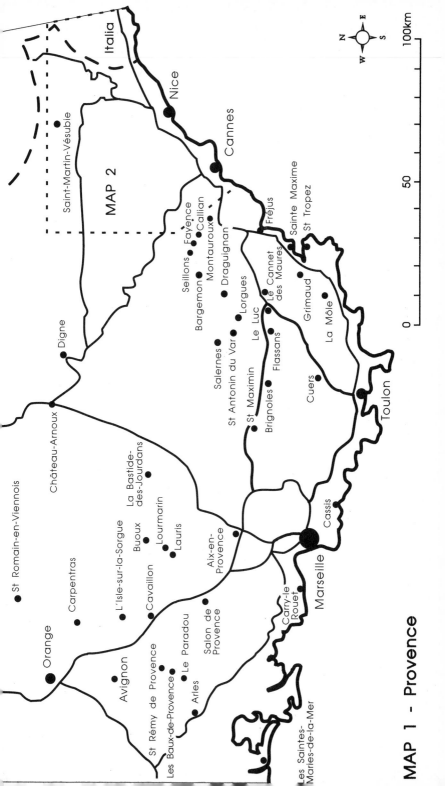

MAP 1 - Provence

Chapter One
ORANGE TO AVIGNON

ORANGE

Driving south, the first major town one arrives at is Orange. It was the site for the Council of Orange in 529 yet much later it became a property of the House of Orange until 1689 when the French eventually took it. It was originally the capital city of the Celtics and called Arausio. It was then colonised by the Romans who left many impressive buildings including a theatre and the only known gymnasium in the whole of Gaul. Nearby the fantastic aqueduct the 'Pont du Gard' carried water from the source of the Eure to Nîmes, about fifty kilometres away. The aqueduct is on the west side of the Rhône so technically it is just beyond the border of Provence.

The town is not known for its eating establishments but the best of the everyday restaurants is opposite the post office and not far from the Roman theatre:

LE PARVIS, 3 cour Pourtoules

Tel: 90 34 82 00. Closed: Mondays except July and August.
Fixed price menus: F98 to F160. Monsieur Berengier.

The owner has created his restaurant in a blacksmith's forge. He has an excellent choice of Châteauneuf-du-Pape wines. His set menus are F98, F130, and F160 so you should spend less than 200 francs per head. His mussel and spinach-filled ravioli are delicious. He also does a lamb roasted in the fire with parsley that is tasty. The restaurant is closed on Mondays except during the holiday period of July and August.

North-east of Orange, near Vaison-la-Romaine, is the small village of St Romain-en-Viennois. It can be found by following the D 71 north-eastward for about 3 km. Here Didier David is the chef and his wife looks after the dining room.

L'AMOURIE, St-Romain-en-Viennois

Tel: 90 46 43 72. Closed: Monday evenings and Tuesdays.
Fixed price menus: F70 to F135. Didier David.

A small hotel with five rooms, this boasts a good country restaurant. There are several set menus, starting with three courses at F70. Then there are five course menus at F110 or F135. There are many choices in each course on all the fixed price menus, and some dishes are included in all of them. My host and I both chose the 70 franc menu.

Looking at the wine list you knew you were really in country France. The choice, not large but ample, started with the house reserve at F35 for one litre, F24 for half a litre. Several Côtes du Rhône wines were priced at F24/38, F24/40 or F30/51. My host chose the bottle at 51 francs as he knew the label. A jolly wine, full bodied and fruity, Domaine de Champ-Long. This red wine is matured in casks.

There was a choice of five different kinds of game pâté as starters. My host chose the pheasant and I the *chevreuil* (venison). We both then had the *civet de lièvre* (hare prepared in a red wine sauce). Very good indeed. We followed with a selection from the cheese board.

While we were having coffee the proprietor came out of his kitchen to talk to us. We talked about game and where he got his produce. He told us most was caught locally and the hare we had eaten had been caught within two miles of the village and weighed over four kilos. I usually eat game only in country areas as they seem to know how best to hang the particular bird or animal and then use traditional recipes in preparing it for the table.

The bill arrived, my host kindly paid it and handed it to me to check the expected total: 201 francs which included the wine, two coffees and service. The water we drank had been local tap, although we had spent the morning visiting 'La Française', a mineral water plant, and 'Ste Cecile', a spring water source. We both laughed about it as we got into the car to return to Avignon.

Food: 8   *Ambiance: 7½*   *Service: 7½*

CARPENTRAS

The bustling town of Carpentras lies in the middle of a market gardening plain. The market every Friday is full of activity, especially during the months between November and March, when truffles are traded.

Carpentras was always of some importance, having been the capital of the Memini tribe of Gauls. As a Gallo-Roman town it was called Carpentoracte. Later, during the period of Papal residence in Avignon, it was capital of Comtat Venaissin. In the lovely old section of town that should be visited, you will find a Roman municipal arch and the oldest synagogue in France. The latter is proof that the Popes in Avignon were dependent on Jewish finance since the Jews were given sanctuary here after their expulsion from France and Provence. The Cathedral of St Siffrein is also worth a visit

The large aqueduct just outside the town was only built at the end of the first quarter of the 18th century. Incorporating forty-eight arches of fifty feet each, it was built for local water.

In town there is a selection of restaurants and most of them do very reasonably priced menus at lunch – around 60 francs for three courses. My choice:

L'ORANGERIE, 26 rue Duplessis

Tel: 90 67 27 23. Fixed price menus: F74 to F188.

Run by two young men, Messieurs Trillat and Pala. A pleasant place with a garden, closing only for Saturday lunch. There is a weekday menu at 74 francs and others at F100, F128 and F188 that are available all week. The wine list is small but gives enough choice.

The most important restaurant in the area is run by a well-known chef, Michel Philibert, and his wife Patricia.

LE SAULE PLEUREUR, *Quartier Beauregard Monteux 84170 about 5 km south-west by the D 942.*

Tel: 90 62 01 35. Closed on Tuesday evenings, except in July and August, and all day Wednesdays.
Fixed price menus: F110 to F295. Michel Philibert.

This is a little pricey with a weekday lunch menu at 110 francs and others at F168, F235 and F295. Worth while for a special treat.

Another 'find' outside town is on the D 4 from Mazan to Apt, then turning onto the D 1:

LE SECRET DES MALAUGUES

This is a place for those who love tranquillity. Set in the middle of a vineyard with a splendid view of Mont Ventoux, this was an old *Mas* (farmhouse) that now serves meals for about 150 francs. They also offer six bedrooms for those who want a peaceful night's rest. There is also a swimming pool.

L'ISLE-SUR-LA-SORGUE

An attractive small town which used to have many mill wheels turned by the river that flows right through the town. Sadly only one remains, covered by moss and often surrounded by people trying to capture it on paper or canvas.

If you are interested in antiques, this is certainly a place to visit. Its several furniture and fine objects hypermarkets are open on

Saturdays, Sundays and Mondays only throughout the year. The dealers, who leave their stands locked up for most of the week, come from far and near, some as far away as Nîmes and Valence. These permanent stands offer mostly country furniture and objects. Yet fine pieces, paintings and objects are also to be found. Fun for a visit over a weekend if you are interested in antiques.

Even if you are not interested in looking for a bargain but find you are nearby you have not wasted your journey. About 4 kilometers outside town on the D 25 travelling eastwards towards Fontaine de Vaucluse, you will find:

LA RASCASSE D'ARGENT

Tel: 90 20 33 52. Closed: Mondays.
Fixed price menus: F65 to F160. M et Mme Norbert Fayolle.

This is really French country cooking at its best. M Fayolle is the chef and Madame does all the serving. She copes unbelievably well with the thirty or so that fill her dining room. There are several set menus starting at 65 francs for three courses, then four courses at F97 or F160. Monsieur buys his fish daily from the fishermen in Marseille. He will make you a *bouillabaisse* (fish soup) but you have to ring him forty-eight hours in advance. He will also do a *paella* but for a minimum of two persons.

There was not a large choice of wine. The local Côtes du Ventoux was 45 francs a bottle and the others started at F50 and went to F130. I chose a half bottle of the local Vin de Pays du Vaucluse, which comes from the Cave de Canteperdrix and costs 30 francs.

As I felt hungry I opted for the four courses at 97 francs. I started with the *soupe de poisson*; Madame brought over a large tureen and commenced filling my bowl. There were also all the trimmings: toast, grated cheese and *rouille*, a saffron coloured mayonnaise flavoured with garlic. We were well in the country so garlic was used generously. I think Monsieur was one that believed it kept you free from colds and the devil. I felt just this portion was going to keep me free from colds all winter and I am sure the devil and everybody else wished to give me a wide berth. No sooner had I finished than Madame was refilling my bowl. I must say I didn't protest. The moment Madame saw my bowl was again dry she was there with the tureen. She was convinced I would be able to enjoy another helping as well as the rest of the meal. I declined and am pleased I did as all the remaining dishes were generous. This is certainly not the place for followers of lean cuisine. I then had a delicious small *dorade* (sea bream) garnished with courgette and sauté potatoes.

I had planned to go antique hunting after lunch, but I was now hoping that one of the stands would have a large bed for me to test. The tray with the cheese arrived and I chose a sliver of *chèvre*, and this was followed by a slice of *tarte tatin*. The latter is my favourite dessert, especially served hot with a ball of vanilla ice cream. It is in fact an apple tart baked upside down with the apples in hot caramelised sugar. When the tart comes out of the oven it is turned over out of the baking dish and all the caramel from the dish flows over the apples and the pastry. I often order this dish and now profess to be a good judge of when it is good. Monsieur Fayolle had a good recipe.

The wine had slipped down easily and I was now enjoying a good strong coffee. The bill arrived: 133 francs. I must say I couldn't complain. I had overeaten; maybe I should have taken the 65 franc menu.

Food: 7½   *Ambiance: 6*   *Service:* 7½

MAS DE CURE BOURSE, Route de Caumont/Durance

Tel: 90 38 16 58. Closed: Sunday evening and Monday.
Fixed price menus: F164 to F258.

If you think you've got a bargain in the antiques market and want to celebrate, drive out of town on the D 25 towards Avignon, then left down a side road to this peaceful farmhouse, or *mas*, for a serious lunch. In summer you sit outside on the terrace by the pool, in winter in the dining room before a great log fire.

Take your pick of Provençal food from a wide range of fixed price menus; for example the F228 *menu terroir* offers six courses of local specialities. They are created by Françoise Donze, who both commands the kitchen and personally discusses the food with you.

On Sunday lunch in winter, I had her delicate *caviar d'aubergines* surrounded by a tomato coulis, and my wife chose the rather richer home-made hot mushroom terrine. We then moved on to *suprêmes de volaille farcis* (stuffed chicken breasts) and *filet mignon de porc* (a delicious pork tenderloin with ginger and honey sauce). Then in place of the conventional cheese board, make sure you order the *chèvre panné* – a fresh round chèvre dipped in egg and breadcrumbs and fried quickly in hot butter. For dessert, Françoise Donze's *gâteau de poire au caramel* is famous, but equally tempting is her chocolate charlotte. The wine list contains a good selection of Côtes du Lubéron (Château de Mille at F116) and Rhône wines.

Food: 8　　　　　　　*Ambiance: 7½*　　　　　　　*Service: 7½*

AVIGNON

When one arrives at Avignon one is immediately impressed by its fantastically imposing walls and monuments. In fact the walls were reconstructed in the late 19th century but the walled town truly captures the spirit of the middle ages. Its prosperity was due to it being at the join of the two rivers, the Rhône and the Durance. The site was a Celtic settlement and then Roman. Little remains of these, as the city chose the wrong side in the Albigensian Wars. The conqueror, the King of France, flattened the defences. During a later stage of the wars the town fell to the Holy Roman Empire.

At the beginning of the 14th century, due to problems in Rome, Pope Clement V, who had been Bishop of Bordeaux, moved to Avignon which he regarded as a much safer part of the Empire. This period saw the city's greatest moments. The Popes built its walls and defences, they also built their palace like a fortress. The city thrived, even after the Popes left and returned to Rome.

Eventually Avignon passed back to France in 1791, having remained part of the Papal States since 1348, when Pope Clement

VI purchased it from Queen Jeanne of Naples, who was also countess of Provence.

The medieval wall is still complete, even with all its restorations, yet sadly the bridge (made famous by the song 'Sur le pont d'Avignon') only goes half way. The first bridge had been built by a shepherd called Benezet, according to legend, on instructions from an angel.

Inside its walls Avignon is certainly much more welcoming. There is plenty to see other than the Palace of the Popes. There are also many good restaurants, some of them very well known. The three top establishments are:

HIELY-LUCULLUS, 5 rue de la République

Tel: 90 86 17 07. Closed: Tuesdays.
Fixed price menus: F170 and F270.

BRUNEL (owner) 46 rue de la Balance

Tel: 90 85 24 83. Closed: Mondays.
Fixed price menus: F140(lunch), to F325.

CHRISTIAN ETIENNE(owner), 5 rue de Mons

Tel: 90 86 16 50. Closed: Sunday dinner and Mondays.
Fixed price menu: F210.

For something much more reasonable in price you should try:

LES DOMAINES, 28 place de l'Horloge

Tel: 90 82 58 86. Open every day.

Here the three TASSAN brothers offer excellent value for money. There is one in the kitchen, another serving the wine and the last running the restaurant. Open till eleven in the evenings.

For a really amusing evening, where the people of Avignon eat, try the Café des Artistes. This can be found on place Crillon near the Porte de l'Ouelle. On this same square you will find the Hotel d'Europe, which has an attractive courtyard and inside lovely antique furniture. The latest owner has spent a great deal of time and money modernising the place without forfeiting its charm. There is also an excellent restaurant. Michel del Burgo is the present chef, who trained with Michel Guérard (the renowned originator of *nouvelle cuisine*), and Ducasse (just awarded three stars in the *Guide Michelin* as the chef of the Louis XV in the Hotel de Paris in Monaco).

CAFE DES ARTISTES, Place Crillon

Tel: 90 82 63 16. Closed: Sundays (ex July).
Fixed price menu: F140. Madame Demery.

Very much a traditional French town restaurant, this has a terrace that is closed in colder months. Avignon can get very cold when the winter Mistral blows. Originally recommended to me by an antique dealer from just outside the city, this is well frequented by the local inhabitants, so there is much bustle with greetings when most customers come in, creating lively activity and noise.

The fixed price menu every evening, at F140, offers three courses, and each course with a choice among five dishes. There is also an *à la carte*. The last time I visited I chose the menu. That particular evening there was a birthday party and the owner had organised two singers to entertain us all. I was on my own but I felt very much included in the festivities.

The wine list has a reasonable choice yet the prices start at F70 and the cheapest half bottle at F50. I do find that pricey. To accompany my meal I decided on a bottle of Bandol Blanc at 70 francs. I wasn't driving as I was staying on the other side of the square.

The service was attended to by a waiter and two waitresses, all young yet professional. The man was in black trousers with a patterned shirt, the girls in the same patterned skirts with black tops. You were attended to not by just one but by all. If, for example, your wine glass was empty any one of them passing your table replenished your wine.

I started with the home-made ravioli, small and light, garnished with parsley and chives. This was followed by *médaillons de lotte* (monkfish) that was beautifully decorated. Served with asparagus and artichoke hearts, the *lotte* was capped with chopped tomatoes and red peppers,the decoration completed with slices of lime. The plate was a work of art, and yet full of gentle flavours. The Bandol with its slightly flowery aroma set the meal off perfectly. I felt I had left enough space to indulge in a dessert: my favourite *tarte tatin* served hot. I did ask for a ball of vanilla ice cream with it. The chef thought it might spoil things so he sent the ice cream on a separate dish.

The wonderful thing when you are served well is that you don't realise the time. The staff had never pushed nor did they clear quickly. They didn't want anyone to feel pressed. With all the other celebrations going on I didn't realise that by the time they served my coffee I had already been there two and half hours.

The bill arrived, what my father use to call *'la dolorosa'* from the term the *via dolorosa,* the hard road. I must say that particular evening I couldn't agree with him. With the menu at F140 and the wine at F70, I also had a mineral water at F15 and a coffee at F8. For the grand total of 233 francs I couldn't feel hard done by.

The guitarists are not a regular feature but are invited to play and sing when there is a large group, or party, or on a Saturday.

Food: 7½   *Ambiance: 8*   *Service: 8*

Chapter Two
LUBERON

CAVAILLON

This town, situated on the banks of the Durance river, first gained power in the celtic period. It was the Greeks of Massalia (Marseille) who then used it as a trading post. At this time the town was situated where the chapel of Saint Jacques stands today. Cabeillio, as it was called, was founded by the Romans on the plain where the town centre now stands. This was in the middle of the first century BC. The Roman arch in the place du Clos dates from one century later but it is no longer in the place where it was originally built.

Since that time the town has continued to prosper as a market centre for the fruit and vegetables that are easily cultivated in the surrounding fields. The market is held regularly and is especially interesting when the famous melons are in season. You can smell them for miles around.

Other places of interest include a good archaeological museum, the 13th century Cathedral that is in Provençal style and a well-preserved 18th century Synagogue.

The town does not boast many notable watering holes. There are several cafés but really not good enough to recommend for a meal. I have stopped here with my family on several occasions. One evening my wife and I ate in a Moroccan establishment – certainly not a meal to remember. I was then recommended to a good restaurant run by a chap called Jean-Jacques Prevot, a notable chef. The next time I went via Cavaillon to Isle-sur-la-Sorgue to look at antiques I booked for lunch.

Easy enough to find on the road going south towards the *autoroute*.

PREVOT, 353 ave de Verdun

Tel: 90 71 32 43. Closed: Sunday dinner and Monday.
Fixed price menus: F139 to F260.

One comes off the busy street into something one wouldn't expect in Cavaillon: an elegant dining room of white and gold and hanging drapes. Spotless and well decorated, one could almost say they have gone over the top and that it borders on a boudoir. I have seen other restaurants in the provinces that give me that feeling, but it is very French.

A large selection of fixed price menus but no *à la carte*. The menus are priced at F139 and F187 for four courses, Then for five courses there is a choice of three menus at F225, F240 or F260. Then the gastronomic ultimate at F350 'a menu of discovery'. I went wild and chose the 187 franc menu. I noticed my neighbour chose the 139 franc menu and his looked every bit as good and as substantial.

The wine list is large with many top quality listings with prices to match. The Côtes du Ventoux AOC at F45/70 is very well priced for this sort of establishment. The Côtes du Lubéron at F68/100 is rather pricey for an indifferent wine. At F40/65 it is, however, tempting to try the dessert wines from Baume de Venise, which is only a few kilometres away.

The dining room is not large as it only seats about thirty. There are two servers, both correctly qualified at one of France's many hotelier schools. They look after your every need and even fill your water glass when it looks empty, without over-filling as so many waiters tend to do these days. Fine quality service that befits fine quality food.

The breads that were offered were all home made: a choice of bread with olives or with walnuts or a lovely wholemeal just a tiny bit warm. I am always tempted to jump in and try several.

The meal commences when an *amuse gueule* is placed before you. This is not on the menu, but offered to start the taste buds working. A good chef always tempts you with something that tickles the palate. This time it was a small *soupe de poisson*, light and delicate, more of a *bouillon*. My choice as opener was *fleurs de courgettes*. Beautifully presented stuffed and garnished with *girolles* (mush-rooms), a stuffed courgette and a stuffed crab. What a flavour! A hint of crab yet plenty of scent from the flower.

There followed a sorbet laced with *marc de Châteauneuf-du-Pape*, to help clear the flavour of fish from the palate. Monsieur Prevot's next dish was *émincée de veau*: veal wrapped in aubergine and topped with cheese, the latter giving a slight Italian flavour. The vegetables completed the decoration. I chose some cheeses from the large tray on offer and decided to decline the dessert, although the desserts looked excellent at the other tables. Coffee was accompanied by chocolates and truffles.

A superlative meal, with plenty of different flavours, yet very well balanced. Monsieur Prevot had a contented client in me. I had not chosen a wine as I had over two hundred kilometres to drive to get back home. The bill arrived: F187 for the meal, F20 for the Badoit mineral water and they had offered complimentary coffee as I had not taken dessert. A total of 207 francs. One can only compliment the chef on his establishment.

Food: 9   **Ambiance: 8**   **Service: 8**

Our next port of call is due east of Cavaillon in the village of Buoux about 10 kilometres north-east of Bonnieux.

BUOUX

AUBERGE DE LA LOUBE

*Tel: 90 74 19 58. Closed: Thursdays. Fixed price menu: F135.
Maurice Leporati.*

A place to go with a group of friends or a couple of families. It is truly Provence country. In fact the restaurant, largely in the garden, is in the middle of the owner's farm. It is all very relaxed and all his dishes are local recipes. There is only one price, 135 francs, and be ready to eat. If you want a small light meal don't book here. If you have teenagers with good appetites this is the place to give them a truly testing experience.

They take your orders for the main course from a choice limited to beef casseroles or lamb roasted with sage. There was also rabbit with mushrooms the day we went. You are then left to help yourself to the great platter of hors-d'oeuvres, brought to your table. Is there a choice? There certainly is – I stopped counting at fifteen.

When you have got through the first and second courses, you can sample a Banon cheese, then dessert, again a plate with three or four samplings for each customer . . . good luck. This isn't the day to slim.

Surprise, surprise. Now the meal is over and you are enjoying your coffee with a sip of *marc*, monsieur Leporati brings out his pony and trap – or is it his horse and carriage? The family do a little show with several horses and carriages. Great fun and a lovely end to a family meal. (You can hire the pony and carriage to take a picnic into the hills, delicacies supplied by Monsieur Leporati.)

The bill ends up at about 175 francs a head. Not bad at all. During bad weather you can sit at tables under the old stable roof or inside, which is quite cosy. In autumn or winter you can find dishes of local game, but it is best to telephone in winter and ask what is on offer.

Food: 7   *Ambiance: 8*   *Service: 8*

LOURMARIN

We now cross the Lubéron mountains and go to the lovely village of Lourmarin: small yet blessed with several good restaurants. The least expensive is:

LE BISTROT, 2 ave Philippe de Girard

Tel: 90 68 29 74. Closed: Thursdays.
Fixed price menus: F68 to F100. Mlle Lescuyer and M Bulland.

However, my favourite is Le Moulin de Lourmarin, facing the old château. Formerly an olive oil mill, very old yet painstakingly restored by the present owners, Jean-Paul and Irene Cahez. There are rooms and these are also extremely comfortable. They have employed a chef, Jean-Marc Goncalves, with impeccable references, who has worked with Paul Bocuse and others of note.

LE MOULIN DE LOURMARIN, rue du Temple

Tel: 90 68 06 69. Closed: 15 November–11 December.
Fixed price menus: F130 to F260.

The first thing to note is that everything is of the highest standard and immaculately maintained. The staff likewise are well trained, some local and others from l'Ecole Hotelier. The mill sits at ease in the corner of the dining room. One can visualise the donkey or mule walking round and round dragging the large round millstone over the olives, crushing them, and the oil oozing out and pouring into the large terracotta pots. The new decoration is in complete harmony with this ancient work place. A true labour of love.

Down to the serious business. There is a week-day fixed price menu at F130 and two others at F160 and F260. The wine list is good, the great surprise being the local Val Joannis which is only 70 francs, so I chose to try it. It went well with the menu at F160.

A lovely meal, well served, but my mind was continually drawn back to my surroundings. I love places restored with taste and quality. I started with the hearts of artichoke and followed with a mixed fish course with a sauce produced from *bouillabaisse*. For the dessert I had a plum tart, a little sharp but I prefer that to very sweet. I am sure if you visit Le Moulin you will agree that it is something special.

Food: 8   **Ambiance: 8½**   **Service: 8½**

LAURIS

Just three kilometres down the road towards Cavaillon you come to the village of Lauris with its magnificent views over the valley of the Durance. Walk along La Roque to enjoy below the patterns of neatly cultivated fields of melons, asparagus or courgettes amongst orchards of apple, cherry and pear. On your right, sharing this view is:

LA CHAUMIERE, *Place du Portail*

Tel: 90 08 20 25. Closed: Tuesday and Wednesday lunch.
Fixed price menus: F198 (weekday lunch) to F265.
Annette Diamant/Julien Corcinos.

Most theatre directors would enjoy such a setting. In the summer you sit out in the courtyard terrace, where swifts wheel overhead in the evening; in winter in the dining room which is cantilevered out from the rock. Both offer a panoramic view from the Mont St Victoire in the east to Les Alpilles in the west, with the Durance river valley between. I have friends who stopped here by chance for lunch, opted to stay overnight in one of the comfortable bedrooms and then decided to buy a house in the village!

Annette Diamant offers an energetic welcome as she discusses what chef Julien Corcinos is busy with in the kitchen. Besides the fixed price business lunch at F198 on weekdays, the main menu at 225 francs offers choices of two main courses, plus cheese and dessert; the 265 franc menu provides a choice of three main courses, plus cheese and dessert. And they reflect the seasonal produce of the valley: thus local asparagus (Villelaure, the asparagus capital of France is just up the road) arrives by April and succulent melons from Cavaillon (the melon capital just the other way) soon afterwards. Julien prepares asparagus in puff pastry and iced melon soup as starters. In summer, we often follow this with fish; perhaps *filet de saumon* with a cream sauce or excellent *lotte*. In autumn, the choice switches to game and locally picked mushrooms. For starters, perhaps a *terrine de lièvre*, followed by *côtelette sanglier* (wild boar) or partridge, pheasant and venison (but watch out for supplementary charges on some items).

Annette Diamant will normally ask for your dessert choices at the beginning of the meal and they are worth leaving room for. The choice includes a light *feuillentine de fraises de bois* or a wafer thin apple tart or delicious chocolate fondant.

The wine list has a wide range of local wines from the home ground of the Côtes du Lubéron, Côteaux d'Aix just over the river, or Bandol and Cassis down on the coast, along with good Rhône wines. Some are quite pricey, but look out for Château La Sable at 95 francs and Val Joanis at 98 francs or the Coteaux d'Aix Château Revelette, whose red wine (here at F98) has been winning a lot of prizes lately.

The bill for all this, if you also have mineral water and coffee, for two people will usually come to around 600 to 700 francs; not cheap, but a memorable experience, especially on a beautiful summer evening.

Food: 7½   *Ambiance: 8*   *Service: 7*

LA BASTIDE-DES-JOURDANS

If you want to explore a little further east to the other end of the Lubéron hills passing the villages of St Martin-de-la-Brasque (which has a lively Sunday morning *marché paysan*) and the beautiful perched village of Grambois you come to La Bastide-des-Jourdans where a good, simple meal can be had at:

AUBERGE DU CHEVAL BLANC

Tel: 90 77 81 08. Closed: Wednesday evening and Thursday.
Fixed price menus: F120 and F190. Agnes and Serge Moullet.

You will spot this small hotel as you drive up the main street. In summer, white wrought-iron tables are set out in the garden behind, in winter you eat in an unpretentious dining-room before a log fire. I suggest you go for the 120 franc menu which is three ample courses. For me, the real surprise was a tasty starter, a bowl of hot artichokes stewed in a white wine sauce with little slices of mushrooms and sausage; almost a meal in itself. The standard main course was fish or guinea fowl, but much better to take the *plat du jour* proposed by Agnes Moullet which was duck and green olives. The dessert choice was rather limited; a pear tart or *crème brulée* (cheese is extra on this menu) . The wine list is rather unadventurous on local wines; the cheapest being Côteaux de Pierrevert at 55 francs, and a small choice of Lubéron wines mostly 75–90 francs. The list is actually much stronger on expensive Burgundy and Bordeaux vintages. With this kind of country food in a Provençal village one would look for a wider choice of inexpensive regional wines. Still, an amiable spot for lunch for two at just over 300 francs.

Food: 7   *Ambiance: 7*   *Service: 7*

We now leave the department of Vaucluse and head due south of Avignon into the department of Bouches-du-Rhône.

Chapter Three
LES BAUX-DE-PROVENCE TO ARLES

ST REMY DE PROVENCE

Set in the middle of fruit and vegetable farms is this fashionable small town. Even though it is fashionable and very residential there are no places of note to eat. There are several that tourists go to but I would not recommend those. The only small lively place is

LE CAFE DES ARTS, 30 bvd Victor Hugo

Tel: 90 92 08 50. Closed: Wednesdays. M. Caritoux.
Fixed price menus: F75 and F90 (do try the frogs' legs).

The town's only famous son was the 16th century astrologer Nostradamus, but its most famous resident was the great painter Vincent Van Gogh, who became a voluntary patient at the Priory of St Paul de Mausole.

We now travel south to a spectacularly rugged and rocky area known as:

LES BAUX-DE-PROVENCE

The lords of Baux ran a powerful and cultivated court, where the medieval troubadours invented the tradition of romantic love in the 13th century. However, their arrogance and later their Protestantism so irritated the French crown that in 1632 Richelieu sent armies to sack the castle and the ramparts. From then on the high citadel of Les Baux has remained a ghost town, but painters, poets and tourists flock to this dramatic peak. Midnight mass is celebrated in the open on Christmas Eve. It was here the words of the carol, 'Noel, Noel' were written.

Since the 17th century the plains below Les Baux have become one of the great olive-growing areas and are now increasingly known for their wines (Coteaux d'Aix en Provence but sometimes billed as Coteaux des Baux). So visitors can enjoy the chance to stop and buy first quality olive oil from local mills in such villages as Mausanne-les-Alpilles or Mouries or directly from estates such as Mas de la Dame (just by the turning up to Les Baux), whose farmhouse was painted by Van Gogh.

Not surprisingly in this setting of outstanding natural beauty, some of the great restaurants can be found. Indeed, one of the most famous in all France, Oustau de Baumanière, tucked into the Val d'Enfer, has drawn appreciative visitors for a generation and spawned a cluster of other good eating-places within a few hundred yards − an example of how a great restaurant lures other chefs to the vicinity.

OUSTAU DE BAUMANIERE, Val d'Enfer

Tel: 90 54 33 07. Closed: Tuesday lunch and Wednesday in winter. Fixed price menus: F550 and F650. Jean-André Charial (chef).

Jean-André Charial is the grandson of Raymond Thulier, the man who created this restaurant and raised it to be one of the best eating places in France. Monsieur Thuilier is still very much involved with the hotel side and its beautiful garden and pool, although no longer the chef. But the great dishes of local lamb and Provençal vegetables such as terrine of aubergines with sweet pepper sauce live on.

The Thuilier family also own, just down the road:

LA CABRO D'OR, Val d'Enfer

Tel: 90 54 33 21. Closed: Tuesday lunch and all day Monday in winter. Fixed price menus: F160 (lunch only) to F350.
Gérard Renébon (chef).

Again, this hotel and restaurant offer a wonderful setting, gardens and food at prices slightly lower than the parent establishment.

Also tucked in this gastronomic valley, beneath the towering crags of Les Baux is:

LA RIBOTO DE TAVEN, Val d'Enfer

Tel: 90 54 34 23. Closed: Sunday evening (winter) and Monday. Fixed price menus: F280 and F420. Mme Novi-Theme.

If you want to splurge on a romantic meal while you are at Les Baux, my recommendation would be lunch or dinner on their terrace in summer. However, the last time we ate here was on a sunny winter Sunday for lunch. In a valley where parking is normally a nightmare, you park peacefully among the trees at one end of the delightful garden.

My wife chose the five course menu at 280 francs and I opted for three courses *à la carte* which in practice was barely more expensive. We both started with a light consommé; hers garnished with tiny strips of duck *aiguillette*, mine with ravioli filled with *écrevisse*. She followed with a salmon trout mousse served with a shellfish sauce. We both had game for the main course; I had chosen venison and my wife's menu included stuffed pheasant. Both were accompanied by a delicate selection of winter vegetables. My wife was then presented with an impressive cheese board from which she selected two different *chèvre* and a slice of *roblochon*, all of which were impeccably mature.

For dessert, I had decided to try out the chef by ordering a hot apricot soufflé at the beginning of the meal. It was sumptuous; full marks. My wife's cold dessert platter included pomegranate seeds, mango ice cream, and dark chocolate cake. From a choice of five coffees, we chose a rich Colombian.

To accompany all this, I had chosen to begin with a half bottle of local white, Mas de Gouronnier, at 70 francs; it proved sturdy and fruity. We followed this with a half-bottle of Châteauneuf-du-Pape specially bottled for the house at 65 francs.

The wine list here is, of course, extensive and can be expensive, but we were most satisfied with these two simple choices. We also drank a bottle of Badoit. The total bill for a lunch that began at 12.30 and finished about 4 o'clock was just under 800 francs. Not cheap, but worth it for a memorable experience.

Food: 7½   *Ambiance: 8*   *Service: 7½*

To complete the tour of Les Baux, I must mention another establishment, high on the crags with a view of the plains below:

MAS D'AIGRET, on the D27a.

Tel: 90 54 33 54. Closed: Wednesday lunch.
Fixed price menus: F160 to F380. Pascale Johnson (chef).

For the kind of food (and price) that you can enjoy every day, venture on six kilometres south to the village of Le Paradou, just beyond Mausanne-les-Alpilles on the D 17 and try lunch at Le Bistro du Paradou.

LE BISTRO DU PARADOU,
Avenue de la Vallée-des-Baux

13125 Le Paradou. Tel: 90 54 32 70. Closed: Sunday.
Fixed price menu: Monday to Thursday: F130; Friday: F140.
Jean-Louis Pons.

The *habitués* who gather at lunchtime in the long bar or the dining room of Jean-Louis Pons' bistro often look like characters from a French movie. Even the patron himself has a slight air of Belmondo. And as old friends greet each other, the drama is often amusing.

Once just after New Year's Day we watched two Frenchmen with rather too ample stomachs approach each other to embrace with good wishes for the coming year. Suddenly they realised the humour of the situation and turned to the whole dining room with the question, 'How do we manage it?'.

In the restaurant, warmed in winter by a huge log fire, each table is set with a carafe of water and of wine from the local Cave Co-opérative. There is one daily fixed price menu for 130 francs, which includes the wine, but nothing is normally written down. 'What is it today?', asks an early arrival. 'It's a surprise,' says Pons who briskly serves the tables himself, while his wife cooks. On this occasion the 'surprise' turned out to be a crisp salad followed by a *pot au feu* of excellent beef and boiled winter vegetables, a choice from a wonderful cheeseboard (including a good chèvre) and *tarte aux pommes* with almond-flavoured pastry. All for 260 francs for two, amidst some of the most entertaining company to be encountered in Provence. On Fridays the restaurant has introduced a special 140 franc menu with *aïoli* (fish and vegetables with garlic and olive oil mayonnaise).

Food: 7   *Ambiance: 8*   *Service: 7½*

We again move south-west to:

ARLES

Here on the western edge of Provence and on the main artery of the Rhône is a town full of history and tradition. This really is old Provence where the local people still dress in traditional costumes on feast days. You will also see much from the past.

Arles is the capital and gateway to the Camargue. Its first name was Theline, given to it by the ancient Greeks. When the Romans conquered the settlement they renamed it Arelate, meaning the town in the marshes. About this time its power grew, as it sided with Julius Caesar in his battles with Pompey. Marseille chose the other side. When Caesar won the Romans made Arles their centre, developing it into an important port by building a canal to the sea.

Economically Arles grew strong and by early in the 4th century AD it was the capital of the Western Roman Empire.

In the town you will see many Roman remains, including statues, columns and the greatest collection, outside Rome, of sarcophagi. There is also a fantastic Roman arena and theatre. The former is still in use today, but now for bullfights, which are generally in the Provençal fashion, where they don't harm the bull. The bull has rosettes attached to his horns. The bullfighters, all dressed in white, are known as *rosetteurs*. Their task is to lift the rosettes from the horns by facing the bull and running towards him. The better the bull the higher the value of the rosette. Both bulls and *rosetteurs* compete in the local leagues. It can be very exciting as sometimes the bull gives chase and the *rosetteur* has to leap the barrier and gain haven in the watchers' gallery with the bull in hot pursuit. It has been known for the bull in his excitement also to jump the barrier.

The Spanish style of bullfights are usually held at Easter and the first weekend of September. These are known as *Corrida Fiestas* and the town is then full. People from all over France, especially from along the south coast, make their way here to participate in the festivities. The restaurants are full and the menus limited, yet very good value for money. The last time we were there we lunched at the:

GRAND CAFE DE LA BOURSE, 22 bvd des Lices

Tel: 90 96 44 73. Open every day.

This is a brasserie serving a large selection of dishes and offering a small selection of hot dishes throughout the day or evening. On Corrida days it offers a restricted menu of different salads, a steak or hamburger and *pommes frites* and *aïoli*. This last dish is a great Provençal tradition, served on bullfight days. It is a white fish served with a large selection of vegetables and garlic mayonnaise. Here you can enjoy the atmosphere and a salad followed by a main dish, washed down with a carafe of house wine and finish with a coffee for as little as 100 francs a head.

The next door establishment, Le Marché, offers *paella*, another traditional dish at this time. Here they prepare the dish in the street. Large dishes about one and half metres in diameter full of rice or the *paella bouillon* (*langoustines*, chicken, calamars, mussels, etc.) are seen cooking away on open gas fires. Here it is still reasonably priced, about 20 francs more expensive than next door. You will enjoy seeing the people dressed in the traditional Provençal prints, and get carried away by the excitement.

Arles has some other good eating establishments. One of the best of these is:

LA COTE D'ADAM, 26 rue du Sauvage

Near the Forum. Tel: 90 93 56 66. Closed: Mondays.
Fixed price menus: F50 to F95. Alain Collet.

LOU MARQUES, 7 bvd des Lices

Tel: 90 93 43 20. Closed: November to 22 December.
Fixed price menus: F200 to F380. Michel Albagnac.

Part of the Hôtel Jules Caesar. It has a lovely garden, a perfect setting for lunch or dinner. The young chef, Pascal Renaud, creates dishes full of imagination and flavour.

LOU CALEU, 27 rue Porte-de-Laqure

Between the arena and theatre. Tel: 90 49 71 77. Closed: Thursdays.
Fixed price menus: F80 to F130. Christian Gimenez.

The great painter Vincent Van Gogh lived here for one year before he died, and in that time completed over two hundred canvases. Driving around the countryside in the midday summer heat you can imagine his paintings before you and of course you will see thousands of sunflowers facing the sun like well-trained soldiers. A wonderful picture in itself.

Make sure you are also in Arles on a Wednesday or Saturday morning since these are market days. Get there early because as the sun rises higher there are more and more people at the same time as the temperature is rising. Here on offer are all the traditional Provençal ingredients to prepare spectacular meals. Try a slice of local sausage or the honey tart – you won't regret it.

Arles,the gateway to the Camargue, lures one to venture forward and south to the capital of this savage marsh land.

LES-SAINTES-MARIES-DE-LA-MER

This is on the flat shores of the Mediterranean sea. The greatest legend for the people of Provence happened here. The story goes that Mary Magdalene, Mary the mother of James and John, the sister of Mary the mother of Jesus, St Maximin, some other Saints and Sarah the black servant girl were set adrift from the Holy Land about fourteen years after the death of Christ. They landed here. St Maximin went to Aix to preach the gospel and became the first Bishop of that town.

Mary Magdalene went to Sainte Baume, where she remained in seclusion until she died thirty years later. There are other stories about her that were bandied about by the Catharts. Her remains were found five centuries later and a magnificent basilica was built to hold them at Saint Maximin, between Aix and Brignoles.

Sarah also became famous as the patron saint of Gipsies. The gipsies congregate here annually on the 24th and 25th of May, when they have large-scale celebrations. They also mass here on the week-end nearest the 22nd October, though not in as great numbers. There is also the 'day of the horse' on the 3rd of June, the time they do their horse trading.

We, as a family, have visited this region several times at Easter. There are supposed to be mosquitoes but every time we have been lucky. In high summer, however, they are plentiful so go prepared with some protection.

Here in these wild marshes you see many small and stocky black bulls, as well as the well-known white horses. Many horsemen in traditional dress still live in single-storey white thatched cottages on the edge of the *marais* (marshes). The wild bird life is amazing and abundant. You are suddenly confronted with a huge flock of pink flamingoes in the sunset and imagine you are somewhere in Africa, certainly not Provence.

When we go to the Camargue we usually stay at the

AUBERGE CAVALIERE ,
about 3 km north of Les Saintes-Maries on the road to Arles

Tel: 90 97 88 88. Fixed price menus: F100 to F180.

This is a very comfortable small hotel built in the local style with large, well-equipped rooms and the sea water just off your terrace. The price of a double room is F550. The dining room is cosy and the food good quality. There are tennis courts and a pool. There is also a small bull arena where occasionally they have a local bullfight. The bullfighting standard here is about five levels below Arles, but you will be invited to try your talent.

There are organised rides out onto the marshes. The whole day is great fun. One rides with a group for about three hours, crossing the Rhône in the process, to the sand dunes by the sea. Here the owner of the hotel has already arrived, scraped the sands for mussels and these, steaks and jacket potatoes are cooking on a fire made from driftwood. Some wine and cheese help to complete the meal. What an unforgettable experience! On the way back, three more hours in the saddle. You can find it difficult and sore, especially if this is your first day galloping back over the sand dunes. But home to a lovely hot bath and a good dinner, you are asleep before your head touches the pillow.

The town of Les-Saintes-Maries is very much what I would call 'seaside', yet its market is so different from what one is used to. There are the usual fruit and vegetables, local cheeses and honey, but also kittens, puppies and parrots. The shops are full of items to do with horses or riding. The restaurants are nothing special. The best place in town is:

LE BRULEUR DE LOUPS, ave Gilbert-Leroy

Tel: 90 97 83 31. Closed: Tuesday dinner and Wednesday.
Fixed price menus: F110 to F205. M. van Hoed.

HOSTELLERIE DU PONT DE GAU,
Route de Arles

Tel: 90 97 81 53. Closed: Wednesday.
Fixed price menus: F85 to F145. M Audrey.

The latter is the better value. One can also stay here for just over 200 francs for a room for two.

We have now completed north-western Provence. On the way back east, however, you might consider a little detour southwards on the N568 through Martigues and on to the autoroute A55 for a quick look at the pretty seaside villages of Sausset-les-Pins and Carry-le-Rouet, just west of Marseille. This is also a handy cut-through to Marseille – Marignane airport. And, if you should wish either to celebrate your arrival in Provence or have a grand finale before leaving, then within fifteen minutes of Marignane airport, you will discover Carry-le-Rouet with its splendid and highly-rated restaurant on the cliffs overlooking the bay:

L'ESCALE

Tel: 42 45 00 47. Closed: Sunday evening and Monday; and early
November to early February. Fixed price menu: none.
Gérard and Dany Clor.

A luxurious holiday mood is set here with pine trees behind, a little harbour below and the Mediterranean sea beyond. Sit down on the terrace and choose from an extensive *à la carte* menu with many sea-food dishes and a bottle of white wine from Cassis. For this privilege, however, expect to pay at least 800 francs for two people and probably rather more. But, if you want to start or leave in style with a memorable meal in a serious restaurant, this is the place to go.

After this detour, we are heading for central Provence by way of Salon, Aix and Marseilles, and thereafter north-east to take a look at Haute-Provence, the other northerly way into this lovely region.

First of all, though, while on the route Nationale 7 a little to the north of Salon, one arrives at a small town called Orgon. Here there is no famous chef or elegant *relais*, but just outside town is Le Fin Bec. This establishment is what is known as a *Relais Routier*. These were small restaurants that offered very good value for money meals, principally to lorry drivers. People realised that the sight of a lot of lorries all gathered at meal time must mean good value, so they started stopping as well, so many of these places had a faithful following. Sadly, for many, the clientele started to dwindle with the building of the *autoroutes*. However Le Fin Bec is a survivor. Here you still have to battle with lorries to find parking space, even on a Sunday lunch time. The last time I stopped for lunch the whole three-course meal cost 65 francs. You won't find much better value for money in the whole of Provence.

SALON-DE-PROVENCE

This is the olive oil capital of Provence. Of course, this wielded quite some punch when olive oil was a very important and expensive commodity. As other oils became more widely used Salon drifted almost into obscurity. Its present claim to fame is its Military Museum. If you are a student of Napoleonic battles this is certainly a must. The museum is one of the best in France.

Places to eat are not plentiful, but you can get an excellent meal for under 100 francs at:

CAFE DES ARTS, Place Crousillat

Tel: 90 56 00 07. Closed: Thursdays.

There is another place a little way outside town:

LA TOULOUBRE

Tel: 90 55 16 85.

This is found by first following the N 572, then turning off onto the D 22 for the village of La Barben. Here in his Provençal *auberge*

Monsieur Rouger produces a selection of excellent local dishes. This is a middle price establishment, about 200 francs for a full meal. During the warmer months one eats on the terrace and on cooler days the homely interior is made even more welcoming by a roaring fire.

If you are travelling south on the *Autoroute du Soleil* and you want to make a stop for a meal you could do worse than stop at the main service at Lancon. This is found south of Salon, literally just after you have paid your toll. This is a large service area with hotel, petrol and restaurants and includes the:

GRILL DE PROVENCE

Tel: 90 42 88 88.

This is in the section that bridges over the motorway (not the self-service) and they have an excellent choice of menus at 85 francs for three courses or four courses for 93 francs.

Both menus offer a help-yourself buffet of hors-d'oeuvres and salad. There are several choices for the main course and as I was having the 93 franc menu I chose the fillet steak. Then a tray of about eight cheeses to choose from plus a variety of desserts to end with. The three course menu allows you either cheese or dessert. A large number of people use this restaurant so this ensures that the salads are always fresh. You will find good and friendly service, clean surroundings, very good food without fancy trimmings. All this on a motorway – where else would you find this?

I travel many miles on *autoroutes* in France and I find this one offers the best quality meals. I therefore often plan to pass here around the time for lunch or dinner.

Chapter Four
AIX-EN-PROVENCE TO MARSEILLE

AIX-EN-PROVENCE

The former capital of Provence is certainly my favourite city in the whole of the south. I have never lived here yet we keep returning. On every visit we find more to please us. Aix-en-Provence has a university and this helps to give an impression that it is young and full of vitality. This city, full of wonderful monuments and records of its historical past, is to me the heart of Provence. It exudes an aristocratic air from its large mansions built during the seventeenth and eighteen centuries.

Aix has a Roman past, and was founded over one hundred years before the birth of Christ. It had been inhabited by the Celtic-Ligurian tribe of Saluvians, and the Romans named it Aquae Sextiae Saluvaiorum, referring to the local hot spring, always of interest to them. This spring still comes to the surface in the moss-covered fountain in the middle of the Cour Mirabeau. It is slightly radioactive, contains minerals and has a temperature of 37 degrees Celsius. The Roman thermal baths can still be found near the Pavillon de Vendôme.

The University of Aix has always drawn great men of letters, such as Mistral who won the Nobel Prize for literature early this century. Aix is also famous for art. Cézanne lived here and painted the nearby Mont Sainte Victoire many times. His studio can be visited, and looks as if the painter had just walked out of the door.

One of the city's main attractions is its music festival which is held from late June to early August. The Festival d'Aix is the opera festival where up and coming stars perform mainly Mozart and early music, and tickets for these professional performances are greatly in demand. The other, Aix en Musique, is a free festival of music that is performed in several locations in the town.

All visitors to Provence should go to Aix and stay at least one night. Sit at one of the cafés on the Cour Mirabeau, sip a coffee or drink and watch the world go by. Whether at noon, shaded by the great plane trees, or on a hazy evening the atmosphere is truly vibrant. The most well-known café, 'Les Deux Garçons', has been the meeting place for artists and intellectuals for over a hundred years. All the streets behind are closed to traffic, so you can stroll and enjoy all the small shops that offer the same choice that you would find in most other French cities. This though is so much more pleasant.

For over five hundred years Aix has been famous for the 'Calissons', a kind of sweet or candy. The main ingredients of this paste are almonds and melons, and it is similar to our marzipan. In Aix it is made into little boat shaped sweets and topped with *glacé royale* or sugar icing. *Calissons d'Aix* are sold in practically every shop. While there you must try at least one.

There are many museums and places of interest and strolling around you will come across many small restaurants. Look at the menus displayed and you will be pleasantly surprised. The meals on offer are generally very reasonably priced. You will also find the quality is good. The wines on offer do not have the elevated prices you will find on the Côte d'Azur. I find no other town in Provence offers such a large choice of restaurants, all excellent value for money. My favourite is:

LE BISTRO LATIN, 18 rue de la Couronne

Tel: 42 38 22 88. Closed: Sunday dinner and Mondays.
Fixed price menus: F70 to F200. Bruno Ungaro.

Young Bruno Ungaro, the cousin of the famous designer, produces extraordinary meals at rock bottom prices. His restaurant is housed in several small intimate rooms on two floors. You will feel at ease the moment you enter.

There are four fixed price menus and an *à la carte* to choose from. We decided the menu at 100 francs, which was '*le menu du marché*' was the one that seemed the most interesting to us that evening.

The wine list also starts at a reasonable price for such a smart restaurant. You can have a Côteaux d'Aix for F35/61, another at 66 francs the bottle. I chose a white Château Lacoste 'Cécile' at 98 francs, which I thought not so cheap for a wine I know well.

Bordonado father and son own this wonderful, large vineyard of Château Lacoste just to the east of Aix. My wife and I visited this lovely property a couple of years ago. Bordonado senior tells a lovely tale of how the property belonged to an ancestor of his, acquired because she was the mistress of the Archbishop of Marseille. Bordonado bought back the property in ruins, thirty years ago. Luckily he found the original plans and rebuilt it exactly as it was. He tells the story so often his son nearly believes it, and his grandchildren certainly will.

For starters we had the *marinée de saumon fraîche au citron* and *la brouillarde aux cèpes* (scrambled eggs with wild mushrooms); there was also on offer *l'entrée du marché* and *les harangs gesier confit* (sharp-tasting conserve of duck gizzards). My guest had the scrambled egg which was just perfect. I had the marinated salmon, which was as tender as the best smoked salmon yet had that wonderful fresh lemon flavour and it just melted in the mouth. The young staff were always attentive, all smart in their black and white outfits. Slim, as they had to run up and down the two floors.

For the main course there were three dishes to choose from: *la blanquette d'agneau*, a *charlotte de sole* with a lobster sauce, (chosen by my guest) and *pot au feu de poulard* which was my choice. I was offered a taste of the sole, which was filleted, firm and meaty and the slight lobster taste from the sauce added that extra aroma.

I finished off my meal with two different goat cheeses, one mature with a lovely sharpness, the other much younger and sweeter. My guest went for a light *crème caramel*. I don't have a sweet tooth, yet I often go for a *tarte tatin* if it is on the menu. We both had coffee. My guest, an Englishman, mentioned how surprised he was at the standard of the food and how well it had been presented. To me this is no surprise as you can turn up in a small village in a backwater of France and have an exquisite meal.

The bill arrived, my 'guest', or so I had thought, reached out and settled it. At my request he disclosed that the total had been just over 300 francs for the two of us, and remarked that one person would be happy to pay this price in London.

Food: 8   *Ambiance: 8*   *Service: 7½*

As I have mentioned before, Aix-en-Provence abounds in places to eat. Here in brief are some others I know that offer good value:

POIVRE ET SEL, rue Constantin

Tel: 42 21 40 73. Closed: Tuesdays. Emmanuel Richy.

LE VILLAGE, place des Tanneurs

Tel: 42 26 07 71. Closed: Sundays.

Offers a good three course menu for under 100 francs.

LA BROCHERIE, rue Fernand-Dol

Tel: 42 38 33 21. Closed: Sundays. Menu at under F100.

This has a patio when sunny and warm, and a lovely fire for those cool or wet days.

LA CLEMENCE, place des Augustins

Tel: 42 27 99 77. Closed: Sunday.

This is just off the Cour Mirabeau. A party of nine of us ate here and were astounded at what good value it was. Mind you, it didn't give all the trimmings, such as linen table-cloths, etc.

The most highly rated restaurant in Aix listed in all the French gastronomic guides is:

LE CLOS DE LA VIOLETTE, ave de la Violette

Tel: 42 23 30 71. Closed: Sundays and Monday lunch.
Fixed price menus: F270 to F380. Jean-Marc Banzo.

LES FRERES LANI, rue Leydet

Tel: 42 27 76 16. Closed: Sundays and Monday lunch.

Recently the two Lani brothers have opened this restaurant in Aix. The Lani family have a hotel with a highly-rated restaurant at Bouc-del-Air, ten kilometres south on the N 8 and D 59. The brothers now alternate between the hotel and their restaurant in Aix. They both cook in a similar fashion yet each has his favourite dishes. Last time we were in Aix my wife and I dined at their new restaurant, a stone's throw from the place des Augustins.

This is a completely new restaurant, decorated to a high standard yet a little cold in *ambiance*. We visited it on a cool evening which didn't help. It is most probably much more welcoming on a hot summer evening. The brothers are young but they have been involved with cooking from a very early age. They have achieved a very innovative style.

They offer two reasonable menus at mid-day, one at 120 francs the other at 150 francs. The latter is their *menu du marché,* plus cheese, dessert, wine and coffee. This is certainly good value as there are no extras. In the evenings they have three menus between F150 and 260 francs.

The wine list starts at just under 100 francs. This I find pricey, especially in areas that have some of the largest vineyards in France. We chose a Ferry Lacombe at 105 francs, a good red very unlike a normal Côtes de Provence. This vineyard is near Trets facing Mont Sainte Victoire. The chap who runs the vineyard did his apprenticeship at Châteauneuf-du-Pape, the vineyards of the medieval papacy north of Avignon.

The staff were young and keen, yet a little rough around the edges. One of them was a young man from New Zealand who had come to Europe on a visit and enjoyed France so much he decided to stay and learn the language. He said he loved Aix.

As it was nearly my birthday we decided to splurge and go for the 220 franc menu. This menu consisted of six courses with no choice. We started with a *mosaique* of foie gras and chicken *suprême* with tiny peppers. Fillets of red mullet in a butter sauce came next as our fish course. I must say this is one of my favourites, as it reminds me of my childhood. Our main dish was *aiguillette* of duck with a touch of ginger. My wife thought this was fabulous as she adores ginger. A good selection from the cheese trolley was followed by a *crème brulée*. The finish was a home-made ice cream of chocolate mint and vanilla-flavoured Normandy cream.

No complaints – or maybe a tiny one. This being a long menu I did feel all the dishes were rich. Maybe we are not as used to this as as the French. The plates were all wonderfully decorated and a well proportioned time lapse was allowed between each dish.

I would advise Monsieur Banzo at Le Clos de la Violette to look to his laurels. The brothers Lani are in town.

Food: 8½   *Ambiance: 7*   *Service: 7½*

We find it hard leaving Aix. We always hope to go back yet there is no *'Fontana di Trevi'* to throw in the coin which will guarantee our return.

We head south to the largest city in Provence:

MARSEILLE

This famous city is the oldest in France; it is also the second largest, and is the largest port. Many books have been written about it so you will find only a brief résumé of the history and its restaurants in this guide. Founded in the middle of the Sixth Century BC by the Phoenicians, Greeks from ancient Ionia on the west coast of Asia Minor, it was named Massalia, and used as a trading post with the Celtic-Ligurians who inhabited the region.

This independent Greek Republic prospered. Later it colonised Nice and Antibes to the east and Agde, near Montpelier, to the west, as separate trading posts. During the Roman civil war it chose to support Pompey rather than Julius Ceasar. When the latter triumphed he immediately set about destroying all of Marseille's defences. The town played second fiddle to Arles until after this was sacked by the Saracens in the tenth century.

It regained prominence early in the middle ages as the main embarkation port for the Crusades. Since that time Marseille has expanded and grown, first as a port trading with all the Mediterranean countries then trading in the last couple of centuries with France's colonies in North Africa and elsewhere. The old port is still in the centre of the city but it is used now for small pleasure craft and local ferry boats. The main commercial port which is over ten kilometres long is to the west.

During the French revolution a local group marching on Paris sang a song, written in Strasbourg by a royalist, that was to become the French National Anthem, 'La Marseillaise'.

The city has a large choice of museums and interesting things to see. The Marine Museum and the Cabinet des Médailles are something special. The latter has an important collection of money starting with Greek coins of the seventh century BC and ending with those of the present day.

As mentioned earlier, the old port is at the heart of the city. In the small streets surrounding the old part there is an abundance of restaurants, many serving the well known fish soup from these parts, *la bouillabaisse*. The authentic dish must be made with at least four different types of fish, one of which must be *rascasse*. If you want to eat the real thing, you look for a restaurant that has a certificate that guarantees the quality. Beware of imitations!

The best restaurant in Marseille is certainly in the Passedat family hotel, Le Petit Nice, on the corniche heading south from the port.

LE PETIT NICE, corniche J-F Kennedy

Tel: 91 59 25 92. Closed: Mondays.
Fixed price menus: F300 to F600. Gerald Passedat.

This is an excellent establishment where Gerald has now taken over from his father, Jean-Paul, in the kitchen. The views are superb, and you can see on the islands spread out before you the Château d'If made famous by Alexandre Dumas in his book, *The Count of Monte Cristo*.

Another two places of note are the Miramar and L'Oursinade. Neither of these is particularly good value for money, but the food is good.

MIRAMAR, *12 quai du Port*

Tel: 91 91 10 40. Closed: Sundays. Fixed price menu: none.
Pierre and Jean-Michel Minguella.

Some of the best fish in Marseille is cooked and served here. Jean-Michel is respected as one of the better chefs in town.

L'OURSINADE, *rue Neuve-St-Martin*

Tel: 91 39 20 00. Closed: Sundays.
Fixed price menus: F195 to F270. Jean-Marie Tronc.

This is in the Hotel Altea, yet an excellent place to eat. Their sea bass done in seaweed is something special.

Certainly my first choice when I go to Marseille is:

CHEZ MADIE, *138 quai du Port*

Tel: 91 90 40 87. Closed: Sunday dinner and Mondays.
Fixed price menus: F100 and F130. Mme Madie Minassian.

Situated on the north side of the port with a terrace in the sun, this restaurant has a great view over the bay. Her fish, the *bouillabaisse* and *soupe de poisson* are fresh and tasty. No fussy recipes or preparations. The fish is cooked with just a hint of herbs. The choice of wines is not large yet very well priced. You will have an excellent meal for under 200 francs.

Another good spot is near Notre-Dame-du-Mont:

COUSIN COUSINE, 102 cours Julien

Tel: 91 48 14 50. Closed: Sundays and Mondays.
Fixed price menus: F140 and F190. Jean-Luc Sellam.

You will enjoy some imaginative dishes. This is an amusing place that offers good value. His wine list is not bad at all and not too pricey.

One could go on for a long time about Marseille, its many fish restaurants and its sights. But this is a large city and it is necessary to be careful as it is not safe like the other towns we have talked about in Provence.

I will tell you a story that happened to us. We had returned to Marseille, this past spring, to collect a piece of a four-poster bed we had bought at an auction. We were driving into town and had to stop at a traffic light. A few moments after we moved forward my wife mentioned that she felt we had a flat tyre. I decided to go forward a couple of hundred yards as we were on cobbles and a hill. Luckily I found a car-rental garage and drove in. We changed the tyre and were told where we could have it repaired. The person to whom we took it pointed out that our tyre had been cut several times with a sharp pointed knife. We were astonished when he asked if we had been robbed. Luckily we had not. Apparently what usually happens is that a group stand on the kerb near your rear tyre when you stop at some traffic lights. Unknown to the driver they stick a knife in the rear tyre, and they usually go for tourists with foreign plates. The driver realises something is wrong as he departs from the lights and stops a hundred metres on. He gets out, unpacks his boot, and while he is changing the wheel he is robbed of suitcase or jacket or something else.

Be alert in Marseille or as some people say, 'remain street wise'.

Cassis

While in the Marseille vicinity, you may want to explore the coast a little to the east towards Toulon. The first place you arrive at is the little fishing port of Cassis which is agreeable in summer and winter, except perhaps on very fine Sundays, when half of Marseille seems to turn up. Cassis is famous for two things: its white wine (the Greeks originally introduced the vine here around 600 BC) and its *calanques*, spectacular fjords cut into the cliffs which you can visit by boat (and in one of which some remarkable neolithic paintings were found in 1991 in a cavern reached by an underwater passage). The pretty waterfront around the harbour itself is fringed with little restaurants, all serving local fish. One of the pleasantest is:

CHEZ GILBERT, Quai Baux

Cassis 13260. Tel: 42 01 71 36. Closed: Tuesday (except lunch June-September) and Sunday evening out of season; January. Fixed price menu: F140. M. Gilbert.

Starters include an excellent *ratatouille* (hot or cold) *soupe de poissons*, or stuffed mussels. There is always fish on the fixed price menus, but if you want to select the best of the day's catch, be warned, *à la carte* can be very expensive.

Food 7½   **Ambiance: 8**   **Service: 7½**

We now head north to look at Haute Provence. This time we are going to enter through the Dauphiné mountains.

Chapter Five
HAUTE PROVENCE

Following the River Durance south from the Dauphiné mountains, one enters Provence at Sisteron. This gateway south was cut open by the river. The Romans were quick to find this weakness in their northern defences and to avoid attack they built a fortification called Segustero. Sadly, little remains of this fortress.

The fate of Provence was sealed here at Sisteron by the Count of Provence, Berengar V who designated one of his daughters as the next ruler. She married Charles of Anjou thus taking her inheritance with her and making this region a part of France.

Haute Provence is very beautiful, with spectacular views and dramatic landscapes. It is very sparsely populated, so the places to stop and savour the recipes of this region are few and far between.

Sisteron itself has no restaurant of note, yet you often see its name on menus all over France. This is due to the lamb of the region that is renowned for its succulence and flavour.

The thing that always surprises me in France is how even in a remote region without many permanent inhabitants you all of a sudden come across a restaurant you would only expect to find near a large city. If you take the A 85 towards Digne you will find one of these at:

CHATEAU-ARNOUX

LA BONNE ETAPE, Chemin du Lac

Tel: 92 64 00 09. Closed: Sunday evening and Mondays.
Fixed price menus: F190 to F560. Jany Gleize.

This eighteenth century coaching inn, set with Provence at its feet, is surrounded by ancient olive trees, cypresses, lavender and sweeping meadows. One can stay in one of its well-decorated and comfortable bedrooms.

The restaurant is stylish, high quality French cuisine with prices to match. Pierre Gleize, father of Jany, opened this hotel and restaurant many years ago. He felt he could cater for the passer-by, who used the *route Napoléon* to enter and leave Provence. His reputation was built by producing excellent dishes using the produce of the region. People passing used to stop and were surprised at the quality, so they would ever after make a point of arriving here in time for a superb meal. Since the opening of the *autoroute* people now come from further afield especially to eat here.

There are many provençal dishes on the five set menus in the price range listed above. These are Jany's favourites. On one occasion when we stopped for lunch after driving south from Geneva, we started with one of their special summer delicacies *fleurs de courgettes farcies aux légumes* – courgette flowers stuffed with summer vegetables blended with garlic and mint, and served with a spicy tomato sauce. We followed this with local roast lamb accompanied by *pommes dauphinoises* served in tiny individual copper pans which, my wife says, were the best she had ever tasted. Then dessert of their speciality *tarte au citron et au chocolat* completed a meal that amply justifies La Bonne Etape's rating as one of the serious restaurants of France with notably elegant surroundings.

The wine list, too, offers a classic selection of the great French wines. My only reservation is that the price of many of the local wines at around 200 francs does seem rather excessive, even in such a grand setting.

All told, you must expect to pay at least 600 francs for two if you choose the least expensive menu, but closer to a thousand francs if you go for any of the others.

The staff are a well-trained team, many of them trainees, from hotelier schools around France, usually the top of their class. The hotels want them as they are good, inexpensive personnel and they want to do their training in the best rated hotels as this is excellent for their CVs.

Food: 9   *Ambiance: 8½*   *Service: 8½*

DIGNE

This town has been well known as a spa since Roman times, renowned for the treatment of rheumatism. The thirteenth century cathedral is worth a visit. The town itself does not give you the feeling of Provence, yet it is surrounded by lavender fields that are famous throughout the world. It is here, every August, that the lavender fair is held. The main hotel houses the best restaurant. The hotel itself was an old convent, so the setting is very attractive. It is also good value if you need to make a stop in the region.

LE GRAND PARIS, boulevard Thiers

Tel: 92 31 11 15. Closed: Sunday dinner and Mondays.
Fixed price menus: F150 to F330. Jean-Jacques Ricaud.

The least expensive menu is offered to patrons only at lunch time. The food is very reliable yet not very imaginative. I have asked myself if they have changed the *carte* at all since I first went there ten years ago. I am most probably being mischievous.

The other place worth mentioning, in town, is a very small inn with a dining room.

LE PETIT ST-JEAN, cours Ares

Tel: 92 31 30 04. Closed: after 9.00 pm.
Fixed price menus: F65 to F130. M. Payan.

Very good value if you don't expect too many frills. But you will
eat well.

If you continue southward on the N 85, after about 18 kilometres you will pass:

MA PETITE AUBERGE, Chabrières

Tel: 92 35 56 52. Open: Lunch only.
Fixed price menus: F70 and F90. Mlle Marchal.

Here you can enjoy a simple meal at a very reasonable price, on
good days sitting on the spacious terrace. Mlle Marchal only serves
lunches, she also closes on Thursdays out of the summer season.

If you continue south on the same road you will arrive at Grasse
and Cannes. This route is tortuous, so please make sure you have
good brakes before you attempt the journey.

Back to Sisteron and head south-west on the N 96 towards Aix.
You can also choose to take the new *autoroute* A 51.

Chapter Six
ST MAXIMIN TO DRAGUIGNAN

Leaving Aix behind us and travelling east we pass the Mont Sainte Victoire on our left, the mountain Cézanne spent so many hours painting. You then pass over a rise and below you come upon a vast plain of vines. You register a town to your right overpowered by an enormous church. This is the town of:

ST MAXIMIN

This great basilica, that dwarfs the town, was started in the thirteen century and built on a sixth century church, according to legend over the remains of Mary Magdalene. St Maximin, the first bishop of Aix, is buried here. The basilica is certainly imposing and is the best example of Gothic architecture in Provence. Sadly it was never finished. Inside it houses a great organ and some wonderful artefacts. Worth a visit.

The organ saved the church during the French Revolution, when it was about to be demolished. Napoleon's youngest brother Lucien later used it as an army depot, and had the organist play the 'Marseillaise'.

The town itself really reminds me that I am in the south. It sits in a plain full of vines, dry and slightly dusty. The market in the central square is always a little boisterous. If you want to feel at home in Provence, take a seat at one of the restaurants in the square in front of the Hôtel de France or the Napoléon. Order the menu of the day and a *pichet* (jug) of the house Côtes de Provence. Wonderful. Both places serve a good meal at well under 100 francs per person.

During the vendange in late September you can sit and watch the farmers driving their tractors towing trailers laden with grapes. They are on their way to the Cave Co-opérative. This is the cumulation of their whole year's work. If they are smiling, the year has been good.

For something better, I recommend:

CHEZ NOUS, boulevard J Jures

Tel: 94 78 02 57. Closed: Wednesdays.
Fixed price menus: F90 to F200. Roland Paix.

From Monday to Friday one can order the least expensive menu and be more than content, in fact be very surprised at the fine quality. All the other menus are available the whole week. The last time I ate there I started with the salad of asparagus and followed it with his wonderful roast pigeon. Most enjoyable.

The next large town, if one continues eastward, is:

BRIGNOLES

The Museum of Local History was the twelfth century home of the Counts of Provence. This was the capital and the town prospered. Celle and Thoronet Abbeys date from that period, and are also worth a visit. There is no restaurant of note in town, but luckily there are two just outside. As you approach the town from the west there is on the south side of the N 7 the restaurant:

AUBERGE LE VIEUX PRESSOIR, route Nationale7

Tel: 94 69 43 07. Closed: Sundays, Mondays and Tuesday evenings.
Fixed price menus: F90 to F150. M Gualco.

The owner is a Cannois of Italian origin. He started the restaurant many years ago and now has his son working with him. He offers good honest food at a fair price. He must be doing it right as his car park is always full when one passes by. He serves between one and two hundred meals most lunch times. Evenings are nearly as busy, but with many more regular clients.

Having chosen a table on the terrace in the sun, my guest and I chose different menus: he went for the 140 franc and I the 120 franc. His starter was smoked salmon and mine melon with the local air-dried ham. His duck *à l'orange* looked excellent and I enjoyed my *coquelet au poivre vert*. Both dishes came with a selection of vegetables

We both decided to stick to mineral water as we had at least two hours more driving, so we chose a bottle of Badoit, which is very lightly naturally carbonated. We had looked at the wine list and were pleasantly surprised – a large and varied selection at reasonable prices. The local *pichet* (jug) was F15/30, that is F15 for the equivalent of a half bottle and the latter for a full bottle. A bottle of the local Pays des Maures was F40. A Domaine 'La Lièvre' Côtes de Provence was F45 and other local château-bottled from that price upwards. Even a good Chablis was only just above 130 francs, so the prices were very fair indeed. We pay so much more when we are on the Côte d'Azur.

The cheese tray arrived at our table as quite a number of people were leaving. We had stopped for lunch at nearly one o'clock, and that is late for the south. They normally finish work from twelve until two o'clock. So plan to start looking for where you are going to eat at around noon. If you don't, you may be disappointed and find everywhere full.

We both had some goat cheese, and I took a piece of blue as well. My guest finished with a fruit Bavarois which he found a touch on the sweet side. I abstained. We both had coffees and asked for the bill. Monsieur Gualco brought it, so we had the opportunity to chat to him. He told us it used to be an old olive oil press and he had converted it into a restaurant. Over the years he had built the business into one that was now very successful. He had chosen to be outside town as he wanted to attract passing traffic, especially salesmen. Now many stopped there at least one day every month. I settled the bill, which was just under 300 francs for the two of us. The great thing in France is that the bill includes service and tax. The only tip they really expect is the loose change, unless of course they have done something special for you.

Food: 7½   *Ambiance:* 7   *Service:* 7½

On the other side of Brignoles, on the route to Toulon (the D 554) at La Celle is another good restaurant. This is a slightly better class of establishment.

LE MAS DE LA CASCADE, La Celle

Tel: 94 69 01 49. Closed: Tuesday dinner and Wednesday.
Fixed price menu: F100 to F280. M Gely.

My wife and I had decided to have a wander around the Var, as this early March Sunday was one of those perfect days we are so lucky to have here regularly in the south. The air was still and the sky clear. In the sun it was extremely hot, yet in the shade there was that winter sharpness.

One of my listeners had recommended this *Mas*. The word means country house, with a capital H, rather than a cottage. I had passed by before but that particular time it was closed. It must have been a Wednesday. The place is set in a dip by a stream and the surroundings are wooded. It must be lovely in summer when one is in need of the shade. One enters a large room with a high ceiling and there is a set of stairs to a mezzanine floor. The room is beamed and a large bar occupies nearly one quarter of it. There are many antique bits and pieces on the floor and walls.

The dining room leads off the bar and is in similar style. Some lovely wrought-iron lights with smaller pieces on the walls and on the tables. The floor was tiled and every table had a pristine white table-cloth. The atmosphere was very comfortable and easy. There are large plate-glass windows at one end that look on to the stream and woods, There are some duck and a goose and, of all things, a sheep. Monsieur Gely, on being questioned about the sheep, told us he had been left there nearly two years before as he had been hurt. The sheep was very content so they had kept him.

As it was Sunday the place filled to capacity quickly, so I was glad we had booked – something I advise you all to do, especially on Sundays, otherwise you may be disappointed. I straight away looked at the wine list so we could enjoy a glass while we mulled over the menu. On our table there was already a bottle of red Domaine des Chaberts, a VDQS from Coteaux Varois. This is the quality below AOC and at 89 francs, I thought high. The local *vin de table* started at 67 francs, which is the price I expect for a Côtes de Provence AOC. I chose the bottle already on the table. It turned out to be a good full-bodied wine with a flowery bouquet: a little sharp yet tasty.

In the week there is a three-course fixed price menu for 100 francs. On Sundays there are two menus, one at 155 francs for four courses and an eight course – yes, an eight course – at 280 francs. The number of courses was not the deciding factor as we certainly were not capable of eating eight courses, however small, and being in the country they wouldn't be small. The four-course menu had a good choice and as Monsieur Gely came to take our order he brought an *amuse gueule*: a *rillettes de porc*, a pork pâté, with squares of toast.

My wife commenced with a *salade tiède de foies de volailles*, a warm salad of chicken livers well presented dressed with a very light walnut oil. I chose an *assiette variée de cochonailles*. This was an assortment of country pork sausages, a little like different kinds of salami. It came with some black olives and gherkins. It was an interesting dish but really too much and I would have been better advised to follow my wife. I always feel obliged to try what most people do not choose.

Our main courses were both excellent, my wife's *dos de cabillaud et langoustine* looked superb, the fresh cod tempering the strong *langoustine* flavour, and the *langoustine* adding colour to an otherwise plain fish. The courgettes and *pommes lyonnaises* completed a very attractive dish. Chefs are becoming more and more artistic with their presentations. I had a *noix d'entrecôte grillé,* a tender piece of beef, bloody in the centre but well grilled on the outside. The same vegetables adorned my plate.

There were about forty of us in the dining room, yet I never noticed that anyone was forgotten. Monsieur Gely and one waitress coped effortlessly. They were always attentive yet never hovering, waiting for you to finish in order that they could whisk the plate away.

There were four cheeses to choose from: brie, tomme, a blue and a chèvre. My wife finds the goat cheese generally too strong, so she chose the tomme de Savoie. I enjoy those with a sharper flavour and had Roquefort. While we were being served with cheese we were asked what we wished for dessert. We had both decided to have the *tarte tatin* when we first ordered our meal, so without looking at the menu we ordered. To our disappointment we were told there was none left. Nevertheless Monsieur Gely rushed to the kitchen and when we had finished our cheese in came two small apple tarts on fine pastry.

It wasn't the *tarte tatin* we were expecting yet it was an excellent effort. We had coffee and Monsieur Gely offered us a 'digestive'. This was a local *marc*, pronounced 'mar', without the final 'c'. Every part of France has one; I find them too strong but many of my wine-making friends enjoy this tradition. Marc comes from the distillation of the skins and pips after the grapes have been squeezed to produce wine. It can be very strong so drink it in moderation if you are not accustomed to it.

Like most Sunday lunches in France, you look at your watch as you ask for the bill and find it is well past four in the afternoon. No surprises with the bill. We had had a bottle of mineral water; the coffees and the wine and the menus at 155 francs. The total came to just under 450 francs. Reasonable? Yes, but I still feel the wine was pricey for what it was. All the other wines were also not attractively priced. This I did point out to Monsieur Gely, when he asked if everything was satisfactory.

Food: 8   *Ambiance: 8*   *Service: 8*

Better than the Auberge le Vieux Pressoir, yet fifty per cent more expensive, but the wine accounted for more than half that difference.

If one leaves Brignoles and heads towards Le Luc on the old N 7 about 17 kilometres from Brignoles or 4 kilometres from Le Luc (after the village of Flassans-sur-Issole) you will see signs for La Grillade au Feu de Bois and antiques. Indeed it is a restaurant with an antique showroom. One of the specialities is old doors beautifully restored.

LE LUC-FLASSANS

LA GRILLADE AU FEU DE BOIS,
route Nationale 7

Tel: 94 69 71 20. Open: every day.
Fixed price menu: 160 francs. M. Babb.

This restaurant was recommended to me by a radio colleague who broadcasts from the Var. I had been staying with Douglas and his wife Jenny, as I wanted to try several restaurants in their area, and also expressed my interest in antiques. They told me I could kill two birds with one stone if I made a stop at this place. I certainly was not disappointed.

You turn off northward from the main road and the hotel-cum-restaurant cum antique business is set about a hundred metres up a private drive. When I entered the lovely large room a lady received me and took me to a table. I must say I was surprised as she was dressed in a twin-set and pearls, something you would expect in the countryside in England, but certainly not in Provence. The dining room looked over the garden. At the far end there was an open fire where the cooking was being done.

I didn't even look at the menu, as on seeing the fire I had decided to have a steak and a salad. I also felt in no need of a drink as the previous evening I had enjoyed a visit to my friends' 'local' in Le-Cannet-des-Maures, (see page 82), so I ordered a bottle of mineral water. I noticed everyone else was enjoying a glass of wine.

The French are marvellous; they can't do without their wine with meals.

A number of the tables were occupied but the place was not full, so Germaine Babb and the lady with the twin-set easily coped with looking after us well. The salad that arrived was huge, in fact it was more than I anticipated. They must have felt I needed feeding up. The fillet steak was superb, that lovely flavour when it has been cooked on the open fire. It came with a jacket potato. I had a couple of cups of coffee as I viewed the antiques for sale in rooms that lead off the dining room.

There is also a large warehouse in the garden which Monsieur Babb kindly showed me. In it there is a range of old doors, singles and pairs, from all periods. If you are restoring an old *Mas* and want some period doors to build in, perhaps for cupboards, this is one of the places to look. (The other is in l'Isle-sur-la-Sourge.)

The bill came, and I knew I had committed an error in not looking at the menu before I ordered. The salad was 60 francs and the fillet steak 90 francs; the total bill came to 185 francs. I asked to look at the menu and noticed the salad I had been given was a full meal one. If I had asked for a side salad it would have been half the price. My mistake! Don't you do the same please. I should know restaurants and usually am aware; I suppose I should have stressed 'steak and salad'. I did notice they had a four course menu for 160 francs, not that I could have eaten four courses. Luckily the salad had been fresh and the steak delicious.

Food: 7½   *Ambiance:* 7½   *Service:* 7½

LE-CANNET-DES-MAURES

Not far east of Le Luc is this former village, now a rapidly growing town, Le-Cannet-des-Maures. The word Maures comes from the large mountain range to the south. Here is a good example where a town, because of its situation, explodes in growth. Avignon did this centuries ago. Le Cannet is situated at a junction of the new *autoroute* and the road to Toulon. Before the *autoroute* this was not important as people headed for Toulon from many directions. Since the *autoroute* it became easier to use this fast road and exit as near as possible to Toulon.

Because of this the town has had a building boom. It is now a centre for research on roses and it has the helicopter school for all military services, where people come from all over the world to do their training. One of the large supermarket chains has its buying department here. More organisations want to come. Michelin are building their tyre-testing roads here, a group of ex-racing drivers are building a race track for vintage cars; the centre for fire-fighting helicopters and planes is being relocated here as well. Twenty years ago this was a small village for the farming community, yet funnily it had a casino before the First World War.

I was staying nearby with Douglas and Jenny so I invited them to their 'local'.

L'OUSTALET, route Nationale 7 (in town)

Tel: 94 60 74 87. Closed: Mondays.
Fixed price menus: F100 and F140. Fernand Ruiz.

Fernand is actually Andalusian and has been here for twelve years, building up this place from very small beginnings. He pointed out all the additions he has done over the years. These have been achieved by offering fine fare at good value. The surprising thing, once you know he is from Andalusia, is that this is a French restaurant not Spanish, but it does have a couple of foreign flavours.

On offer are two menus: one at 100 francs for four courses and the second comprising five courses at 140 francs. There is an *à la carte* as well. Surprisingly there is a good selection of fish, which the patron pointed out he had bought himself.

The wine list did not disappoint – a good selection of local wine fairly priced. The *vin du pays* F17/28, vin du Var F45, a Côtes de Provence AOC F34/55, and Domaine de Saint Baillon, from nearby Flassans, at F42/72. A reasonable Bandol was priced at very little more. There was also a choice from other regions. I left Douglas to choose, as he and Jenny have their own vineyard, and he opted for a good Côtes de Provence red and the white Domaine de la Bastide Blanche at Bandol.

We were extremely well looked after. I am sure it wasn't only because my guests knew the patron well. Jenny commenced with the *bouquet de crevettes* (fresh prawns) and followed with a *filet de sole à la champignon* (sole with mushrooms). Douglas took the *galantine de canard* (pâté of duck) and the *civet de lièvre* (jugged hare). I decided to take the 100 franc menu as it looked very tempting. I wasn't displeased. The *soupe de poisson*, then *moules farcies* (mussels done like stuffed snails with garlic and butter), and as a main course, yes you read correctly, I had the *dorade* (a lovely piece of sea bream). There was a small supplement of 10 francs for this.

We decided to turn down the cheese and go straight to the desserts. I am glad we did, just to see Douglas's face when his *profiteroles* arrived: his eyes were watering. Jenny had the pineapple with kirch and I a sorbet of *cassis* (blackcurrant).

Monsieur Ruiz mentioned that during the winter months he generally had game on the menu. This was due to his own interest in hunting. He went on to describe his present expansion plans, which consisted of building a fifty-room hotel a couple of hundred metres down the road. One must raise one's hat to him.

It was well past midnight when I requested the bill. What a lovely surprise to find that for the three of us it was under 550 francs! This is one of the attractions of the Var; feasting at reasonable cost.

Food: 8   *Ambiance: 7*   *Service: 7½*

We now head north of the *autoroute* and the *route nationale* 7 and really get to the heart of the Var. We are going to visit Salernes, St Antonin du Var, Lorgues and Draguignan.

SALERNES

A really surprising small town of three thousand inhabitants, thirty kilometres west of Draguignan on the D 560, mostly involved in pottery or tile making. This is the place for tiles from Provence. If you are restoring a house or wish to re-do a bathroom or kitchen, and you want to use tiles, this town is a must. There are fifteen factories, some that make the tiles by hand using the original wood burning stoves; others much more automated and modern.

GRAND HOTEL ALLEGRE, route Principale

Tel: 94 70 60 30. Open: Every day.
Fixed price menus: F55 and F85. Famille Allègre.

My wife and I had been visiting several tile manufacturers in the town. At lunch time one advised us that they were closing until two o'clock, and told us if we wanted lunch to go to this hotel.

When we entered we were impressed by the largeness of the dining room with the sitting area at the far end and a log fire that is burning most winter days. A high beamed ceiling is set off by a huge mural on one wall. This depicts monks tasting wines in a cellar and enjoying themselves. It is slightly formal but friendly. You are led to one of the tables set with lovely crisp table-cloths and napkins.

You are handed a menu and you will be surprised. There is a set three course meal with no choices at 55 francs, and another with a choice of three dishes per course at 85 francs. There is also an *à la carte*.

The service was performed by two waitresses of 'a certain age'. Everything well presented in the traditional manner. My wife and I were browsing over the menu when we noticed our neighbours being served. We were immediately tempted and ordered the same. My wife had the *coquilles St Jacques* and the *brochette d'agneau* for me. We started with a *salade de chèvre chaude* and *crudités* respectively. All these were chosen from the *à la carte* menu. The main courses were garnished with *pommes Dauphinois* and a very light spinach flan.

The wine list was just as tempting. A *pichet* (jug) of the house wine was priced at F8/15, a Coteaux Varois which is VDQS at 33 francs the bottle, a Côtes de Provence AOC Domaine Thierry at F34/54. This vineyard is on the road out of Salernes towards Draguignan. I must say it is very hard to find restaurants that will offer you wines at these prices. We had a small *pichet* of *rosé*.

We chose not to have dessert, even though the tarts on show looked appetising, but we did have coffee. The bill, even though *à la carte*, came to 217 francs.

I did eat here on another visit to the tile manufacturers, this time on my own. I had spent the morning choosing tile seconds as we wanted to create an impression of old tiles. These are well fired tiles with slight imperfections sold at a very attractive price, but you have to pick them yourself.

Having worked hard I returned to the hotel. This time I had already decided to have the 55 franc menu.

The dish that day was a *terrine de canard* (duck pâté) followed by *côte de porc* with *pommes purées* (mashed potatoes). Several fruit tarts were again on offer and this time I chose the pear, home-made and delicious. Coffee and a half bottle of mineral water pushed the bill to a mighty 80 francs.

I left, very content, ready to face more tile selection. The sun had been hot all morning yet this January afternoon you could still see frost in shaded corners. They say these strong frosts in winter help to strengthen the vines.

Food: 7½   *Ambiance:* 8   *Service:* 7

LORGUES

During one autumn, my daughter Carla came down for a visit with her boy friend and they both expressed an interest in visiting a vineyard as it was about the time of the *vendange*. We arrived in Lorgues at the Co-operative as loads of grapes were being literally poured into the machines that squeeze out all the juice. The supervisor straight away takes a reading of the sugar content, and tells the farmer the information, as well as the weight of grapes delivered. From this each farmer knows what his income will be from the harvest. South facing slopes generally produce higher sugar content which will determine the alcohol level.

At noon all work came to a stop. We headed into town to the:

AUBERGE JOSSE, *avenue de Toulon*

Tel: 94 73 73 55. Closed: Monday.
Fixed price menus: F60 to F125.

This was a simple country place, yet there were linen napkins and table-cloths. It was quite a large restaurant and could seat over a hundred. It seemed to be the place that catered for local functions; not very attractive from the outside, but cosy inside.

There are three fixed price menus on offer. Three courses at F60, four courses at F95 and 125 francs for five courses. We came to an agreement that we would have a light supper but a good lunch. Alex and I chose the 95 franc menu, but Carla wanted frogs' legs so she chose *à la carte*.

The wine list was just as inexpensive; their *vin de table* at 12/18/29 francs for 25/50/75 centilitres; that means a bottle at 29 francs. The Côtes de Provence Ste Beatrice was at F37/55. We chose a Cuvée des Princes at 55 francs. A good wine that maybe lacked a little in body, yet had a good bouquet.

Back to the meal. My daughter started with the *cuisses de grenouille*, followed by *magret de canard aux olives* (fillet of duck breasts). This was served very pink and was as tender as butter. Alex and I did very well choosing the fixed price menu. He had *cochonailles* (five different sorts of pork) then *crêpe aux cèpes*, followed by a steak and *pommes frites*. He is a growing boy so needs lots of meat. I had a *terrine de maison*, an *omelette au champignon* and then *pintade aux haricots* (guinea fowl). I must say I don't often have guinea fowl but how succulent it was and the flavour so much better than chicken.

We all had desserts. I was cautious and had a vanilla ice cream. Carla (no stopping her!) a chocolate mousse and Alex an apple pie. Two of us had coffee. The bill was just over 400 francs for the three of us. My daughter's meal came to more than half again of our menu price. She only had three courses and we had four. It just shows how the fixed price menus are such good value.

Food: 6   *Ambiance: 7*   *Service: 7*

Also in the same town:

LE FOUR, rue Vieille Commune

*Tel: 94 73 79 96. Closed: Mondays. Fixed price menu: None.
Pascal Boullée.*

Again this is a restaurant that serves good wholesome country fare. Sadly no fixed price menu, but all the dishes are reasonably priced. As you know, I prefer a menu as this helps you easily to calculate the cost of your meal as you order.

Le Four is in a back street. On entering with a couple of friends I was surprised to see it was quite full, with a mixture of locals and foreigners. In fact there were several nationalities. A lot of people obviously know of this as a place that serves a reasonable meal at a good price. We really cheered up at seeing it so well supported. The person who recomended that we come here knew what he was talking about.

You can have a hot starter for between 22 and 30 francs, and cold starters for 15 to 38 francs. Main courses F56 to F85 and a choice of pizzas for under 40 francs. Looking around one could see the portions were of a good size, and certainly when our dishes arrived we were not disappointed.

The wines were also keenly priced, with a 25 cl *pichet* at F7, 50 cl at F14 and a litre at F20. I had a taste and it was certainly drinkable. There were other wines ranging from a *vin de pays* at under F40 to a Côtes de Provence AOC at F45. My hosts felt they wished to taste something a little better, so we had a bottle of Ste Beatrice at 60 francs.

My hosts both chose the *salade de saison aux croutons grillés* with garlic. They judged it fresh yet nothing special. I had a lovely tomato salad with a good dressing and some basil leaves to add that extra flavour. The main courses were much more successful. My hostess had veal cooked in breadcrumbs, my host grilled lamb chops which he found perfect and I had the *entrecôte* grilled with herbs. All the dishes came with super *pommes frites* and a side salad.

The service was done by Pascal Boullée and one assistant, who found no difficulty in coping with a full restaurant that seated around forty. The original ordering had taken some time, but we had been the last but one table to arrive. Once they had taken our order our meals were served without too much time between courses.

We had double espresso coffees each, and the bill when it came was no shock: a total of 360 francs. So our meal averaged out at 120 francs each.

Food: 7　　　　　　　*Ambiance: 6½*　　　　　　*Service: 7*

The easiest way to find the next village is to go through Lorgues and follow the directions for:

ST ANTONIN DU VAR

This is a lovely small village lost in the middle of vineyards. In late autumn, when the grapes have already been picked, you will find the leaves on the vines turning to exciting reds and oranges. The surrounding country is ablaze with colour. It matches in many ways the Indian summers of northern New England in the United States, and Canada.

The restaurant is in the middle of the village. It looks onto the playing fields of the village across which are the village church and the wine Co-operative. You also catch a sight of the vines.

LOU CIGALOUN, *in the village*

Tel: 94 04 42 67. Closed: Tuesdays.
Fixed price menus: F75 to F175. Denise and Jean-Pierre Chevraux.

You enter through the bar which has that well used look, yet very clean and tidy. The dining room is long , with beams, and many farm implements hanging on the walls. There are other country pieces littered about. The impression is almost that you are in some friend's country place, except for the size.

The cheaper menu is only available during the week. I visited with a colleague on a Sunday in November, so we did not have the opportunity to try this menu. The other two menus were both of five courses at F125 and F175. We felt we were not in need of five courses so we turned to the *à la carte*, which I do not often do.

The wine list gave us a pleasant surprise. We presumed that the prices were so reasonable because it was one of the village bars. They offer their house wine at F9 for 25 cl, F18 for 50 cl and F34 for the litre. There were other local wines at 38 francs and a Côtes de Provence at F30/50. Wines from other regions were also on the list at acceptable price levels. We decided to have one of the better Côtes de Provence, a Sainte Roseline; not cheap at 85 francs.

We chose as starters *brouillade de truffe*, very finely scrambled egg with pieces of truffle, and a home-made *terrine de sanglier* (wild boar pâté). The *brouillade* was 'exquisite', I was told. On the other hand I was not too impressed by the terrine, I found it to be rather heavier than I enjoy. Luckily I had chosen *pageau* (small sea bream) as a main course and this I found to be light and full of flavour as it came with rice and a saffron sauce. My guest had a *magret de canard*, which has become very popular in the last ten years. Both were thoroughly enjoyed.

If you are preparing a *magret* or breast of duck at home make sure it does not come from a duck that has been fattened especially for its liver. This is the advice of a friend who is a chef in the Périgord. My wife and I were in Brive market one morning, and purchased a couple of *magret*. We were advised to cook them very briefly in the frying pan, just a few minutes either side on a hot fire. Then we were told, 'before you take them from the pan pour on some strawberry vinegar and let it take the fat from the duck'. We tried it and it was delicious. Before then I knew nothing of strawberry vinegar.

We both had two cups of coffee and we had also drunk a bottle of mineral water, yet the bill was a little more than I had bargained for. It came to nearly 500 francs. The scrambled eggs with truffles were quite pricey. Next time I will come back hungry and have the menu.

Food: 8　　　　　　　*Ambiance: 7½*　　　　　　　*Service: 7½*

Onwards to the former capital of the Var:

DRAGUIGNAN

Restaurants and hotels in town have been well marked by the local Mairie to help everyone find their way.

LOU GALOUBET, *boulevard Jean-Jaures*

Tel: 94 68 08 50. Closed: Sunday dinner and Monday dinner.
Fixed price menu: 98 francs. Mme Michel.

This was recommended to me by one of my listeners, and I made a special trip to Draguignan. Although Toulon is now the main city of the Var, luckily for Draguignan it still has all the local government buildings, built at the end of the last century. The *Sous-Préfet* of the *Département* – the latter is the equivalent of County – operates from here. The main business of this region is wine.

The menu at just under one hundred francs had some good choices. As starters there were *salade provençale, soupe de poisson* or *moules marinières*. The main course offered a choice of *sardines escabeaux*, rumpsteak, *roulade de veau* or *assiette de coquillages farcies*. Then you could choose between cheese or a dessert.

The wines were a little pricey but the list had great variety. The least expensive was a local wine at F58/98, a Côtes de Provence was F60/98. For two of you this comes to about the same price as the menu.

Madame Michel, the owner, led me to a red leather banquette. There were few people already in the restaurant so I moved to face the main dining area. The whole place reminded me of restaurants I used to go to in the late fifties and early sixties with my parents. You see a lot of this in the second cities of France and Italy.

Madame took the order and the young waiter looked after all of us in a formal manner. I had ordered the *moules* to start, and a large serving dish was brought and placed at the table next to me. A bowl was filled and placed before me leaving ample in the dish for a second helping. which he duly served me with when I had finished.

For the main course I chose the rumpsteak, which came with potatoes and spinach. The same performance was re-enacted. One does not come across this mode of service very much these days. Twenty years ago this was standard practice. Even the great restaurants now place your plate before you complete with all the trimmings.

I finished the meal with apple tart, followed by a coffee. I had not had wine as I had a long drive in front of me, but I did have a bottle of mineral water. The bill was no shock at just over 120 francs. Two with wine would be in the region of 350 francs, which I think is excellent value considering the quality, quantity and the way the meal was served. Those with large or small appetites will be content. Sadly Draguignan is not just round the corner for me.

Food: 7½   *Ambiance:* 7   *Service:* 8

We will stay north of the *autoroute* until we reach the Alpes-Maritimes, then we will return and deal with what is south of the motorway including the coast of the Var.

Going east from Draguignan along the D 562 towards Grasse you go close to a series of famous perched villages. To reach them you must deviate slightly north on the narrow, twisting D 25 and then the D 19. the villages are Bargemon, Seillans, Fayence, Tourrettes, Montauroux and Callian. These were the six Roman fortress cities, each one sited on the summit of mountains and in visual communication with the others. Some originated earlier than the others, but only came to prominence during the Roman occupation. Their histories since then have been entwined, yet often one found them supporting opposite sides during the wars.

They have now become fashionable places to live. Generally the houses in the villages are small, but they have spectacular views. I list the villages with some of their points of interest and a restaurant you will find pleasant for a stop.

BARGEMON

This is the furthest west; its central square, the heart of the village, has some elms and a fountain. The parish church dates from the fourteenth century.

AUBERGE PIERROT, place Ph–Chauvier

Tel: 94 76 62 19. Closed: Sunday dinner and Mondays. Fixed price menus: F60 to F250. M Pierrot.

SEILLANS

The oldest of the six villages perches around its feudal château and has an eleventh century church. The town elders sealed the town during the plague of 1580 so none of the inhabitants were affected. It is now in the forefront of the perfume trade and it also specialises in the production of corks.

AUBERGE MESTRE CORNILLE, in the village

Tel: 94 76 87 31. Closed: Monday dinner and Tuesdays. Fixed price menus: F100 and F165. M Barthe.

FAYENCE

Only the remains of the château of the Bishop of Frejus are left. The streets and the large square are often used for antique fairs, or *Foires de Brocante*. The lovely church in the square is thirteenth century. From here you have a splendid view of the plains below, with an airport used by gliders. The Dukes of Savoy occupied the town in the fifteenth century, during the wars of religion. We have been coming here for twenty-five years and often eat in the:

FRANCE, rue du Château

Tel: 94 76 00 14. Closed: Wednesday evenings and Thursdays.

The dining room is very cosy for cool days and winter evenings and there is a small terrace for the warmer season.

LE POELON, rue Font-de-Vins

Tel: 94 76 21 64. Closed: Sunday dinner and Mondays.
Fixed price menus: F90 to F150. M Dupas.

TOURRETTES

The château du Puy dominates this village, but it was only built in 1830, and is still in private hands. The original château de Villeneuve was destroyed by the people of Fayence during the wars of religion. There is no real restaurant of note in this village.

MONTAUROUX

Here in the square next to the church, reapers used to thresh their corn. Look at the frescoes in the Chapelle St Barthélemy – they are outstanding. This church was rebuilt in 1635 having been destroyed by the Duke de Epennon in 1592. Early this century it was owned by Christian Dior, but on his death he gave it to the community. Christian Dior also owned the Château Fortress, about three kilometres away, which dates back to the thirteenth century.

AUBERGE LA BECASSIERE, on the N 562

Tel: 94 76 43 96. Closed: Sunday evenings and Mondays.
Fixed price menus: F90 to F180. Jean-Charles Tirinnanzi.

This is situated on the N 562 between the turnings to Callian and Montauroux. The area is called Le Plan Oriental. The restaurant itself is an attractive *Mas* with creepers over most of the front of the building. I went with a Canadian godson and his girl friend who were both attending Nice university at the time.

The interior dining room is used only on cold or wet days. We were lucky to be there on one of those lovely warm late April days. We sat on the back terrace surrounded by a beautiful leafy garden full of mature trees, and were served by Madame Tirinnanzi, capably assisted by a waiter and a waitress. I was very surprised to find how quiet it was, the main road being on the other side of the house.

Madame mentioned that Monsieur was hard at work in the kitchen, but during the hunting season he escaped at every opportunity. You can find whatever he has shot on the menu a few days later. I made a note to return in the autumn.

Unusually, for a restaurant in the country, they had a tank full of *langouste*. Madame mentioned that they had regular clients living nearby who enjoyed fresh shellfish but did not want to travel too far. This was the reason they had installed the tank. Now many of their summer visitors see the tank and decide on the spur of the moment to enjoy a lobster.

There were three menus: F90, F125 and F180. My godson, wishing to try the duck *à l'orange*, chose the expensive menu; his girlfriend and I went middle of the road. We also ordered a bottle of Les Demoiselles from Domaine Ott at 70 francs. There were other less expensive local wines starting at F40/65.

My godson having ordered five courses demonstrated how an American football player can demolish them almost without taking breath. His meal started with smoked salmon, then prawns in garlic, his first taste of duck *à l'orange*, cheese and to finish chocolate mousse. As he was in Nice for a year I got to know how much he loved his chocolate mousse. His girl friend was much more reasonable. She commenced with a *salade gourmande*, this is with *pâté de foie de canard*. Her main choice was turbot in a light cream sauce. I didn't know her well enough to ask for a mouthful. She had some brie from the cheese board then strawberries and cream. My meal was most enjoyable and I think quite well balanced. I started with *moules farcies*, excellent strong flavoured, garlic-stuffed mussels.

Steak *forestière* in a cream sauce with wild mushrooms. Then cheese and a strawberry tart.

We all had coffee and we laughed at Madame's comment when I had asked, at the beginning of the meal, for mineral water. She was not going to serve me mineral water as the local tap water was much better than anything we would find in a bottle. She saved us a few francs and she had been right; the tap water was clear, fresh and tasty.

Lunch had cost under 500 francs for the three of us.

Food: 8 **Ambiance: 7½** **Service: 7½**

Close by just off the N 562 is another lovely inn. This one is truly well in the country. To find it, start at the cross-roads of the D 562 and the D 37, just south of Montauroux, and go west about 2 kilometres on the D 562. Look out for Clos St Bernard and a stone works, where there is a sign to the inn to the left on a tiny road south. After several kilometres you will come to:

AUBERGE DU PUITS JAUBERT,
route de Lac de Fondurane

Tel: 94 76 44 48. Closed: Tuesdays.
Fixed price menus: F155 and F210. M Fillatreau.

If you love tranquillity, then this is one of the places to make for, in the heart of the country. Also you can stay here and on my first visit we looked over the rooms. They were very comfortable with private bath, yet terribly reasonably priced. In fact some rooms were better priced than the menus, but you do get a beautiful meal.

Originally I had been told of this inn by a friend. We had driven all the way one cold evening from Monaco, had dinner and returned: a good hour's drive each way. I hadn't realised it was so far. I ate there recently with my brother and his wife and found it was still good.

The owner had originally made some money in business and bought this fifteenth century *bergerie* and made it into a small hotel cum restaurant. His son, Henri, then trained with some of the best as a chef. A place like this needs one of the family to acquire experience in the kitchen or in hotel management.

The setting helps to create the atmosphere. There are two long stables with vaulted ceilings, side by side. In between is a large open fireplace. It is all stone and wood. Beams cross the flat ceilings. The walls are very thick so it remains cool in summer. There is a lovely terrace for those that love the sun. The setting is idyllic.

The food is also excellent. The wine starts at as little as 55 francs for the local product. We chose a Côtes de Provence at 60 francs. Really, not a bad price.

The service is done mainly by the family, and when needed they bring in several helpers from nearby villages. On this occasion two of us had the fixed price menu and my brother went for the *à la carte*. Two of us started with the smoked salmon, smoked in house and tender with a lovely flavour, a slight touch of pine. My brother had a *salade Landaise*, which contains small pieces of well grilled ham. His main course was a *tournedos*, a large portion of tender beef cooked to perfection. My sister-in-law had *grenadine de veau*, a fillet of veal with grapes and a grenadine flavoured sauce. I really enjoyed my *rognons au moutarde*, kidneys in a creamy mustard sauce. Each dish was accompanied with courgettes, *sauté* potatoes and a couple of half tomatoes with a touch of breadcrumbs grilled under the fire.

Cheese to follow: a large assortment to choose from, with some local cows' and goats' milk cheeses. The two of us eating from the menu had a *feuillette de poire*, a feather-light pastry with pears. My brother, to be different, had hot apple tart with vanilla ice cream. I am sure he needed to diet after this meal!

Excellent quality in very welcoming surroundings are hard to beat. The price, a touch over two hundred francs each. We had coffee all round and it included a couple of bottles of mineral water.

Food: 8½   **Ambiance: 7½**   **Service: 7½**

The last of the perched villages is:

CALLIAN

The village fountain is fed by a spring that was developed by the Romans when they were building the aqueduct for Fréjus. The château is of twelfth century origin, and it was recently restored, having been left abandoned for many years. There are a couple of reasonable eating establishments in this village, yet to my surprise both are closed on Wednesdays. One would have thought that they would organise themselves a little better.

LE PETIT VATEL, place Honoré Bourguignon

Tel: 94 76 40 55. Closed: Wednesdays.
Fixed price menus: F90 to F220. Mme Rebuffel.

The room is simple in style and decoration yet the view of the local countryside, through the windows, is splendid. Stick to the lesser priced menus and you certainly won't be disappointed.

AU CENTENAIRE, rue de Lyle

Tel: 94 47 70 84. Closed: Wednesdays.
Fixed price menus: F68 to F130. M and Mme Martellino.

Small and cosy but in mid-summer the tables are too close for comfort. Yet it is unbelievably good value for money. When I eat there I wonder how they can make money. Monsieur Martellino is from St Etienne and it was there he did all his training. He called the place Au Centenaire as one of his uncles celebrated his hundredth birthday in 1985 just after he had bought the restaurant. He is in the kitchen with an assistant and his wife does the service assisted by one girl.

The menu at 68 francs includes a *pichet* (jug) of wine and three courses. What do you think of that? There is another three course menu at F95 and the 130 franc menu has four courses. The wines start at 45 francs and there is ample choice.

We had eaten a good lunch so we just had one dish for dinner. My guest chose a fillet steak with *gratin dauphinois* potatoes and salad, I a steak tartar with *pommes frites*. Both were well prepared and simply served.

Being seated close to the other tables, I found it easy to chat to the people near me. On one side were four English people who had eaten the two cheaper menus. They all thought it was excellent value, and mentioned how surprised they were to eat three courses with wine for only 68 francs. On our other side was a Frenchman, who regularly ate here when he was at his holiday home. He had been a hot air balloonist, competing in two French Championships, and had just taken up gliding. He did this from the airport at Fayence. Apparently the expert can take off in the morning, catch the thermals and go all the way to Mont Blanc returning by evening using other air currents. They sometimes reach 8,000 metres. WOW! I have always been tempted but have never had the courage.

Back to Monsieur Martellino's restaurant. We had drunk a Côtes de Provence Château Kennel that had cost 70 francs, a bottle of mineral water and four coffees, in all 260 francs. The steak tartar was excellent, and that is test enough for any restaurant. If you are in the region, do try it out.

Food: 7½   *Ambiance:* 7   *Service:* 7

We will now wander back to Le-Cannet-des-Maures and proceed south to the coast, then work our way along the coast to St-Tropez and then the famous Côte d'Azur.

Chapter Seven
TOULON TO FREJUS

Leaving Le-Cannet-des-Maures we head south on the N 97 towards Toulon. Just over half way is the small town of;

CUERS

LE LINGOUSTO, *route de Pierrefeu*

Tel: 94 28 69 10. Closed: Sunday dinner and Mondays.
Fixed price menus: F195 and F350. Alain Ryon.

I found this place purely by accident. I had been to Toulon, in search of old doors. One of the reasons I was able to create this guide was that I was occupied in restoring an old property and it led me all over the region searching for the different pieces I needed. On my way back from Toulon I spotted just off the motorway a place selling stone gates, fireplaces and other pieces recovered from old houses. As I needed a stone fireplace, I made my way there. It was nearing noon and the owner was ready to shut up shop. I quickly looked around and as I was leaving asked if there was anywhere in the vicinity for a reasonable lunch. I was advised to visit Le Lingousto. 'You won't be disappointed,' he told me.

On arrival I was more than a little surprised to find a lovely new building in local style. I looked at the menu outside and nearly left. Then I thought again and went in. You really would not expect to find a dining room like this in the middle of fields of vines. Very elegant and formal, the tables were set with silver glistening in the sun on superb pink linen. The staff, dressed in formal wear, were standing upright as if on parade. A young lady, who later I found to be Madame Ryon, led me to a table by some french doors and handed me the menu.

I had been surprised by the price of the fixed price menus posted outside, but now I was more greatly surprised to find *haute cuisine* in this nondescript village and that here in mid-week I secured the next to the last table available. Having been open-mouthed on entering, I was further astonished by the food. I asked Madame Ryon if it was normally as full. 'Oh yes,' she said, 'we are full most days and most evenings as well'.

Because it is not in the village you do not pass it by chance. You have to cross the railway tracks and take the road to Pierrefeu for about two kilometres. I asked how they came to be there. She mentioned that the Mayor of Cuers (he was actually sitting at the next table) was a regular visitor to a small restaurant they had been managing in a little village nearer Toulon. He found Alain to be an excellent chef, schooled by Georges Blanc and Roger Vergé, and the Mayor wanted a superb restaurant in his village. The Mayor arranged for the land to be made available and planning permission, and they then borrowed the money and built. The restaurant has only been open since 1989. So if you want to do something in France, you must impress the mayor. They are very powerful people.

I chose the 195 franc menu. I ordered a beer and a bottle of Badoit since I had a good couple of hours drive to get home. The wines, as you would expect in such a place, are pricey and start at around 100 francs for a Côtes de Provence.

Having ordered the menu a small plate arrived, adorned with what they call in France an *amuse gueule*. This is a tempter to get your taste buds going. This happened to be a *quenelle* – a mousse of vegetables – light and delicious. The beginning of a wonderful meal. I ordered asparagus, followed by the *tournedos* of veal.

I was astounded when the plate of asparagus arrived. It was beautifully decorated, there is no other word for it. First there was ample asparagus, not like some of the *nouvelle cuisine* offerings. Second, the decoration consisted of herbs fried in very light batter. A large mussel rested on a bed of mashed potatoes and a small potato had been hollowed out and filled with anchovy. You had a fantastic mixture of flavours that left the palate quite looking forward to the main course. I nearly weakened and ordered a bottle of something to complete this wonderful interlude, but I restrained myself.

The *tournedos* of veal, when it arrived, was as beautifully prepared and presented. The veal was accompanied by a pouch of pastry filled with chopped mushrooms, and tied up with very fine tender *haricots verts*. Next to these some *pommes dauphinoises* and a *tranche* of courgette stuffed with ratatouille.

I finished my meal with a cream cheese matured to perfection. I had eaten the same cheese, a few days before, in a two-star restaurant in Toulouse, and there was no comparison. I am sure Monsieur Ryon will soon be awarded his second star by the *Guide Michelin*. I had some coffee and prepared to pay the bill. I had a good journey ahead of me to continue savouring a very special meal. The experience had cost under 250 francs with no wine. I am sure two could do it for about six hundred if you kept to this menu and chose a local wine.

Food: 9   *Ambiance: 8*   *Service: 8½*

From the above you can see that I have rated the whole experience very highly. This restaurant is something like an oasis in the desert, that is the area between Le Cannet and Toulon. Alain is what the French call a *'chef très sérieux'*. I call him bloody good.

TOULON

It is such a contrast to go to a small town, practically a village, and find a restaurant which will certainly hit the heights, and then go to a large town like Toulon and find they have nothing to compare. There are a couple of places worth mentioning, for those that get stuck there and need to find somewhere reasonable to eat:

LE DAUPHIN, rue Jean-Jaures

Tel: 4 93 12 07. Closed: Saturday lunch and Sundays.
Fixed price menus: F132 and F192. Alain Biles.

It is a restaurant without warmth yet Alain Biles produces some excellent dishes, including a ravioli stuffed with snails. You can eat well for between F200 and F250 depending on how you order.

LA CORNICHE, littoral Frederic-Mistral

Tel: 94 41 39 53. Closed: Sunday evenings and Mondays.
Fixed price menus: F130 to F290. Chef Eric Berthier.

Monsieur Berthier is certainly well qualified: he trained with Loiseau and Guérard, the latter being the originator of *nouvelle cuisine*.

The rest of the coast has restaurants but really nothing that I would go out of my way for. You need to go east as far as La Mole to find something special.

LA MOLE

AUBERGE DE LA MOLE, in the village square

Tel: 94 49 57 01. Closed: Mondays.
Fixed price menus: F125 and F280. Rene Raynal.

Rene Raynal, the owner, is a small, lively gentleman very like Napoleon, and seems to run his restaurant in similar manner! Everything is run very efficiently. You arrive there, just off the main road, to find a square with a lovely terracotta painted church all edged by plane trees. On that same square is the Auberge.

You walk straight into a bar, the local village bar, and then you walk into and through the kitchen, believe it or not , to the restaurant. On your way, you can check what Monsieur Raynal's son, who is now the chef, is preparing for lunch. The dining room, when you eventually get there, harks back a little to yesteryear, with posters of the grand epoch of travel showing great ships bound for Brazil and the French colonies, trains to Carcassone, Rodez and other lovely names that were tourist resorts when our parents were young. A lovely fire at one end adds to the warmth of the decorations.

My wife and I arrived with our younger daughter, who lives in America, and our son. We arrived rather late on a wet Sunday lunch time. Monsieur Raynal said, 'Don't worry, its no problem, there is plenty to eat for everyone'. How right he was. The two menus are very far apart in price. The first is served only at lunch and frankly if you are successful in eating that and wanting more you have a much larger appetite than I. The second menu offers several more courses, that include frogs' legs and omelette with wild mushrooms. We all chose the 125 franc menu and I am sure if you follow suit you will be more than content.

The lovely thing is that you only have the main course to ponder; all the others will be placed before you and you help yourselves. That day the main course offered a choice of *magret de canard*, *faux filet*, *confit de canard* or *gigot d'agneau*. My wife chose the duck *confit* and the two youngsters had the *magret* of duck while I decided on the *gigot* (roast lamb).

I was then handed the wine list. On the first page there was an assortment of local wines and Côtes de Provence at prices ranging from F46/80 for a half or whole bottle which was not cheap. I ordered a bottle of Côtes du Rhône and a glass of white for my daughter, as that is what she prefers. I then casually turned over the page and to my surprise saw a long list of the best known wines in France. A list you would only expect to see in the best hotels and restaurants in the world. Château Latour, Château Margaux were among those listed. There were wines in his cellar dating back to 1936, well over fifty years old. The prices were higher than what we had ordered but not expensive for what they were. An example was a Château Latour 1966 at 2,600 francs: you would certainly pay more in a restaurant which is rated.

The dishes started to arrive. First a large basket of fresh country bread, and then four large terrines and a huge jar of pickles. A good forty centimetres high jar contained gherkins, cauliflower, pimentos and onions. The terrines — a *rillette de porc*, a *pâté de volaille*, a duck pâté and another country pâté. You were expected to help yourself, and they didn't mind if you finished the dish. They never hurry you. Please do not over-eat the first course as you will not be able to enjoy the courses that follow.

By this time Monsieur Raynal was seated at another table chatting to the customers. He spent most of the meal visiting each table seeing that everyone was content. He explained he now left the cooking to his son, and he was only there to make sure his customers were satisfied.

The main course arrived. The *magret* that our children had chosen looked as if they had a whole breast of duck each, tender, sliced thinly and pink. My daughter found it was too much and left nearly half but my son had no problem finishing his (he was still in the middle of his rugby season). My wife's *confit de canard* was just as tempting, and I was very pleased with my *gigot* of lamb. The French cook lamb much less than we do, so that all remains pink, and I now prefer it this way. Though I do miss the mint sauce. All the dishes were served with *sauté* potatoes mixed with *girolles* (wild mushrooms). Absolutely delicious, a recipe of Raynal senior.

As soon as we began our main course they placed a large bowl of green salad on the table. When we had finished the salad there was a lovely *plateau* of cheese — five choices — a Roquefort, another blue, I think it was the Auvergne, a Cantal and two cream varieties. The final onslaught was the desserts — again several dishes were placed on the table to help yourself. On offer were a large dish of *crème caramel* beautifully prepared, a bowl of stewed prunes, another bowl of pears in red wine, and lastly a dish with a chocolate and coffee ice cream *roulade*.

Now you know why I warned you not to help yourself to too much of the first course. I also asked myself how others could order the larger menu! We had coffee. It was nearly five o'clock yet the restaurant was by no means empty. We had started late, but a meal like this is not an affair to hurry. I got the bill, for the four of us just over 650 francs. A very reasonably priced feast.

Walking back through the bar to leave, the son showed us photos of his own son who had just had his christening all dressed up in a chef's *toque*.

Food: 8   *Ambiance: 8½*   *Service: 8*

You can have a stroll afterwards in the square, it is very rural here. Or you can drive on to the picturesque perched village of Grimaud which is not very far.

GRIMAUD

I am going to describe two restaurants in this hill village situated on top of a hill above Port Grimaud, the well-known modern fishing port designed as pastiche Riviera, not far from St Tropez. First I will mention the highly rated restaurant you will find listed in all the gastronomic guides:

LES SANTONS, *route Nationale*

Tel: 94 43 21 02. Closed: Wednesday.
Fixed price menus: F300 to F480. Claude Girard.

However, I want to pay more attention to a place you will not find in most of the guides but which I would rate the best in the area. It was recommended to me by some friends who have a holiday home in Port Grimaud. They did say it was not cheap but that it was something special. If you have something to celebrate, and you are nearby, this is the place to come.

LA BRETONNIERE, *place des Pénitents*

Tel: 94 43 25 26. Closed: Sunday evenings.
Fixed price menu: F325. M Rabud.

My wife, son and I had been invited by a New Zealand friend to spend Easter aboard his yacht. We had gone to St-Tropez, where he had found it difficult to get a mooring on the central quay.

Luckily he was very friendly with Madame Senequier, who owns the famous café Senequier, and she organised that we should be moored right in the centre of the quay amongst all the great yachts. Another couple were also guests aboard. I invited my host, his guests, Monsieur and Madame Senequier and their daughter Katherine to dinner on Easter Saturday. Monsieur Senequier declined as one of the family had to look after the café. So with Katherine's car and a couple of taxis we headed for Grimaud.

We arrived at the restaurant in the place des Pénitents, certainly the place to be if you wish to do some penance in comfort. You are greeted by the owner who seats you at table. I was very surprised to hear that Madame Senequier had not been, although she mentioned that her husband had eaten here with a group of friends but she had not as she had been ill at the time. She was thrilled to have the opportunity to try it out now as he had told her it had been excellent.

The restaurant is beautifully decorated in the traditional style of Provençal *Mas*: stone, beams and panels of mature honey-coloured wood. The ceiling is high with half the seating area on a mezzanine a few steps up. As one enters one finds the restaurant abounds with flowers. Beautifully decorated tables are set with linen and lace table-cloths and finely starched napkins. There were more flowers on each table. That evening there was a central display of tulips at least a metre across. The whole restaurant was warm and welcoming but flowers make it so much more alive.

The owner is rotund and cheerful. He runs about taking the orders then back to the kitchen to do the cooking. He has two very professional servers, but wants to make sure everything is as you want it.

The menu includes an *amuse-gueule*, two starters, the main course, cheese and dessert. The last is his *pièce de résistance*.

The wine list was a very pleasant surprise. In places such as this you expect the cheapest wine to start at around 150 francs, but here it starts with the local Château de Tours de Grimaud at 60 francs a bottle. He advised us to try the red which 'we find excellent otherwise we would not put it on our list'. Excellent it was. I also ordered a Sancerre, for those preferring white wine, a fair price as well at 120 francs.

Please do not eat much lunch if you intend to dine here. One excellent course followed another. I will describe only what I ate. I started with fresh green asparagus, hot with a cold vinaigrette sauce, firm but well cooked throughout. Each stalk could be eaten completely. I find the green has much more natural flavour than the white. There was then a sorbet to clear the palate. I then had the *mignon d'agneau* (lamb fillet) flavoured with honey and pepper. This gave a bitter-sweet taste which I enjoyed. Beautifully done. The cheese trolley was huge and full of choice and he likes you to try at least one variety. Then the dessert. This lavish display on two trolleys is something for the eyes to behold. The night we dined there, there were sixteen different desserts. Monsieur Rabud serves this course himself. Desserts are the love of his life – he just adores making you try one after another. We all ended up with at least three different desserts on our plates.

Everyone said they had enjoyed the meal tremendously, and looked forward to trying it again as they would be more prepared to do justice to the cheeses and desserts. The bill came to just below 400 francs a head. A few of us had drunk an apéritif, we had five bottles of wine, six bottles of water, six coffees and a couple of *digestifs* at the end. For the quality, the number of courses and our liquid consumption I feel it was excellent value.

When the bill arrived I was a little shocked. It wasn't the total price that hit me but that the restaurant **did not accept credit cards**. Only cash or cheque. When I told him this had surprised me, he said: 'now that I know you – if you don't pay to-night, I expect a cheque in the post in the next couple of days'. Luckily I did have a cheque with me.

Food: 9   *Ambiance: 8½*   *Service: 9*

If you want to avoid disappointment I must advise you to book. There were a couple of tables spare and people came in to see if there was a table available but they were refused. Obviously he takes bookings up to a certain number by a particular hour and then stops. He then prepares the food to suit that number of people.

Go and try it; I am sure you will enjoy the food and the atmosphere and find the owner welcoming.

The other restaurant I know in Grimaud is very different from the one I have just described . This next one is in the place Neuve, from where you can get a spectacular view of the plains below.

LE CAFE DE FRANCE, place Neuve

Tel: 94 43 20 05. Closed Tuesday.
Fixed price menu: F105. M Darras.

The last time I ate here was with my son Andrew. We had been looking at a sixteenth century stone fireplace just below the village, and as it was a lovely day we decided to have a little wander about and have lunch.

The restaurant is situated on this lovely square, and you can easily park your car in the middle under some plane trees. On hot days this keeps the car cool. The restaurant has a long terrace that faces the sun. If you want to get a sun-tan even in winter, choose a sunny day and go and sit right up against the restaurant so you are out of any breeze, and have lunch. Like so many family restaurants in France, this offers straight-forward well prepared meals served with efficient politeness.

The menu at 105 francs is not cheap, but you get four courses. To start with we had a *pâté maison* served with a few gherkins and a *salade frisée aux lardons*. The *frisée* is that lettuce that is light green in colour and looks as if it has been in curlers. Both of us followed this with a grilled *entrecôte* steak and the inevitable *pommes frites*.

You are well looked after by the owner's wife, his daughter and two other helpers. The wine starts at F40/60 which I find a little high for this sort of restaurant, and they do not offer a *pichet* of house wine. We both had a slice of the brie which was just beginning to ooze, and finished off with fruit salad for me and chocolate mousse.

We sat there getting warm and brown, sipping our coffees. The terrace was full as I am sure it is most days, so if you are going for lunch book or get there early. The price of our lunch with a bottle of wine came to just under 300 francs. That I feel is a little expensive for lunch. You get a similar-priced menu at dinner and that I feel better value. That may sound ridiculous but in France it is expected to pay less at lunch. Most restaurants offer three courses rather than four.

Food: 7½   *Ambiance:* 7   *Service:* 7½

There is another small place that only serves Italian dishes at reasonable prices;

LA SPEGHETTA, montée Saint-Joseph

Tel: 94 43 28 59. Closed: Mid-week in winter.
Fixed price menu: 85 francs. Fabien de Paz.

The next resort is always a must on the itinerary of any visitor to the Côte d'Azur, from Easter to November. During the summer months St-Tropez is hard to get into by car. Sometimes the road there is jammed and when you get to the town it is even harder to find a parking space. Many also pour in by boat. You will find them moored five deep from the quay.

ST-TROPEZ

The name St-Tropez comes from a legend. The Christian Roman Centurion Tropez was beheaded by order of the Emperor Nero in Pisa. The legend goes on to recount that the two parts of him were set adrift in a boat with a cock and a dog, who were expected to devour him to satisfy their hunger. In fact they left the corpse alone and an angel guided the boat to what is now this popular resort.

Very similar legends are recounted at Saintes-Maries-de-la-Mer and Monaco, the former celebrating and the latter concerning a young girl called Ste Devote.

At the end of the fourteenth century St-Tropez was destroyed during one of the many wars. In 1470 a Genoese, Raphael de Garezzio, with sixty families, was given permission to settle there by the Grand Seneschal of Provence. The former offered to re-build and defend it on condition they did not have to pay tax. One of the original tax havens. It became a small Republic headed by the original families, later led by two elected Consuls and twelve Councillors. They had an army and a navy and after 1558 there was a Captain of the town, elected annually.

The Republic lasted until the seventeenth century. The people were always at the ready, rebutting the Spaniards and the Turks. They helped neighbouring areas, and helped Sourdis, Archbishop of Bordeaux, to recapture the Islands of Lerins from Spain.

The statue on the quay is Judge Admiral Pierre de Saffren (1726-83), one of France's greatest sailors.

Two great festivals occur annually. The first is the religious procession on 16th and 17th May in honour of the patron saint. The population is armed with blunderbusses with muzzles that flare out like horn; these are fired and get a response from naval submarines and torpedo boats, sent specially for the occasion. The second festival, on 15th June, is a remembrance of 1637 when twenty-two Spanish galleys attempted to take the town, but were sent packing by the town militia.

Early this century St Tropez was a submarine port. During the second world war it was an area chosen for one of the Allies' main landings. It really did not come into prominence as a resort until Brigitte Bardot came to live there and put it on the front page of most newspapers in the late Fifties. Even though it now gets extremely crowded the town centre has retained its charm.

The best way to view St Tropez in mid-summer is from the rear deck of one of the lovely yachts that are ever-present on the quay. Most of us are not so lucky, so the alternative is to sit on the terrace of the famous café Senequier. It is in the centre of the old port on the quai Jean-Jaurès. Here at one of the rich red-coloured tables and matching awning one can view the world, and easily spend all day doing it. The café is open for breakfast at about eight in the morning and stays open till the last group of customers leave, sometimes as late as two the next morning. A visit to St-Tropez without a visit to Senequier's is like going to Rome without a visit to St Peter's.

The café serves wonderful croissants produced in their own *pâtisserie*, which you can visit in the street directly behind. Here you can buy not only croissants but a wonderful selection of cakes.

The Citadel is situated on a small hill above the town. From here you can view the town, the bay itself with Port Grimaud at one end and across the Gulf to St Maxime. Behind you across the peninsular you can see stretching westward Pampering beach with its famous names – the 55 Club, Bora-Bora and Tahiti. This is where to spend the day sunbathing and at noon lunching at one of these restaurants. They are expensive but you will be mixing with all those names that make the front pages of the tabloids.

Back in town you can eat dinner at one of over a hundred restaurants, some in the back streets and others on the quay. It is difficult to say this or that restaurant is good value, as St-Tropez is a swiftly moving scene. Walk around town looking for those that please you and looking at the menus. None are cheap. If you want to be on the quay, a restaurant that has been there a long time is:

LE GIRELIER, quai Jean-Jaures

Tel: 94 97 04 47. Closed: 1 January to 15 March.
Fixed price menu: F160. M Rouet.

This is a large restaurant which offers a wide selection of dishes. It is well maintained and efficiently run. The numerous waiters and waitresses look after you in a friendly and helpful manner. It fills quickly in the evenings and at lunch at week- ends. Do not expect to get out of here for less than 250 francs per person. The advantages are that the food is fresh, it is in the middle of the action and you can eat at your leisure.

The last time I lunched there I had *moules marinières* followed by a *dorade* with boiled potatoes and a fine runny mayonnaise sauce. Very good.

Food: 7½   *Ambiance:* 7½   *Service:* 7½

Many of the better restaurants are attached to hotels, and a number of these are on the various roads that lead out of town. The most highly rated is:

CHABICHOU, *avenue Foch*

Tel: 94 54 80 00. Closed: 10 October to 15 May.
Fixed price menus: F280 and F500. Michel Rochedy.

On the route de Gassin is:

LE MAS DE CHASTELAS, *quartier Bertaud*

Tel: 94 56 09 11. Closed: end October to Easter.
Fixed price menus: F300 to F400. Racine and Sulitzer.

The restaurant in this eighteenth century country house hotel really has no set menus, but the price of the whole meal is set by the price of the main dish.

Another in St-Tropez itself has a great following among stars and celebrities:

LE BARON, *rue de l'Aioli*

Tel: 94 97 06 57. Closed: Tuesdays.
Fixed price menu: F380. Gerard Chauvet.

If you leave St-Tropez and take the road to Port Grimaud then you come to:

SAINTE MAXIME

This is also a sea-side resort, but it does not have the cachet of St-Tropez, so prices are much more attractive in its restaurants, though it has many fewer. The best is:

L'AMIRAL, le Port

Tel: 94 43 99 36. Closed: Sunday evenings and Mondays.
Fixed price menus: F150 and F210. Henri Guerre.

A good value establishment is:

LE DANIELE, avenue G-Leclerc

Tel: 94 43 96 45. Closed: January.
Fixed price menus: F105 and F155. M Lemarquis.

Onwards along the famous coast to:

FREJUS

The town is built on a rock plateau about a mile from the sea, lying in a plain between the beautiful hills of the Esterel and the Maures. It was founded by Julius Caesar, in 49 BC and takes its name from 'Forum Julii', as a stop on the historic Roman trade route the 'via Aurelia'.

In 31 BC Octavius, the future Emperor Augustus, made it an important naval base. Here he built his light galleys for the war against Anthony and Cleopatra. He also retired his veteran soldiers to this area, giving them Roman citizenship, money and land. This helped the town to develop quickly into a city of 25,000 people. An aqueduct was built to bring water from twenty-five miles away.

There are many Roman remains, including parts of the naval base, which was twenty-two hectares (52 acres) in size – very large for that time. At the south quay you can still see one of the towers that guarded the entrance to the port. At that time they closed the port at night by raising a large chain that lay between the two towers. Here, also at the entry to the port, you will see the Lantern of Augustus.

The Romans also left the aqueduct, theatre, the oldest arena in Gaul, the wall, Gaul gateway, the military headquarters (called 'the platform') and the golden gateway.

With the long Roman peace the military port slowly lost importance until at the end of the second century AD the fleet was removed entirely.

From the time of the Romans until the tenth century Fréjus existed quietly. The Baptistry in the Episcopal city is from the late fourth century, one of the most ancient in France. In the tenth century the Saracens destroyed the town and in 990 AD Bishop Riculphe began rebuilding the modern city. Once again it became a large naval port in the reign of Henri II, but many sailors contracted fevers from the nearby marshes. Eventually during the French Revolution the port was sold to private owners, who filled it in.

The cathedral dates from the tenth century and the Episcopal Palace is now the town hall – the Hôtel de Ville, or Mairie. The town has grown again with the influx of tourists, and so has the town nearby, St Raphael. It is no longer obvious when you leave one and enter the other.

The main feast of the town is the third Sunday after Easter, when they celebrate St Vincent de Paul whose statue is carried through the town on a boat. The whole town is involved in this huge celebration. If one is in the region it is worth a visit. So is the following restaurant:

LOU CALEN, rue Desaugiers

Tel: 94 52 36 87. Closed: Wednesdays. Fixed price menu: F170.
Francois and Annie Gallione.

This small establishment is situated at the side of the square where you find the church and the town hall. Madame welcomes you into a small intimate dining room which, apart from the nine tables themselves, could be a dining room in her home. She and her husband do everything for their restaurant, shop, wash and iron, clean, cook and serve. They have had the restaurant for a dozen years and are very welcoming.

The delightful surprise is a menu at 170 francs comprising four courses, the first two offering a choice of five or six dishes. The wine list also is not expensive, starting at F40/75 for a Côtes de

Provence from Le Luc. We chose another Côtes de Provence from La Motte at 80 francs.

Annie Gallione hands you the menu then very clearly explains what they have prepared for this meal. She then returns a few minutes later to take the order. I found her very easy to understand.

I ordered something different as a starter, a *tartar de saumon à la infusion de citron*, minced raw salmon mixed with herbs and lemon juice, absolutely delicious. (A few years ago if you had offered me raw fish I would have quickly turned up my nose in refusal.) My guest chose a *fricassée de volaille fermier aux moules*, again an exquisite dish of chicken and mussels, unlikely partners. Our main courses were no less remarkable, my guest having *mille feuille* of Auvergne trout with wild mushrooms and I a *gourmandise* of sole and St Pierre on a bed of saffron rice.

We enjoyed a little moment to savour what had passed and to anticipate the dishes to come. We were not disappointed. The cheese was a roundel of goat cheese that Madame took from a large jar, pickled in olive oil with herbs and spices. For dessert a *tarte tatin* of pears was served, unusual to me as I had always had this made with apples.

With coffee Madame lingered and told us she was originally from Brignoles and her husband from Toulouse. They had a fifteen-year-old daughter who helped a little during the school holidays and they generally closed the restaurant during the school autumn half-term, to visit family. The bill with the wine and coffees came to 440 francs which struck me as even better than when I first saw the price of the menu.

Food: 8½ *Ambiance: 8½* *Service: 8*

The best drive along to the Alpes Maritimes or its coast, the Côte d'Azur, is by the coast road. Here with the red stone of the Esterel mountains on your left and the dark blue sea on your right, the road curves following the shore line. You pass small villages and the odd country house, as this is the last area between St-Tropez and the Italian border that isn't over-populated and spoilt. This is the French Riviera as it used to be. Savour it while you can; the next time you visit you may find building cranes along the horizon.

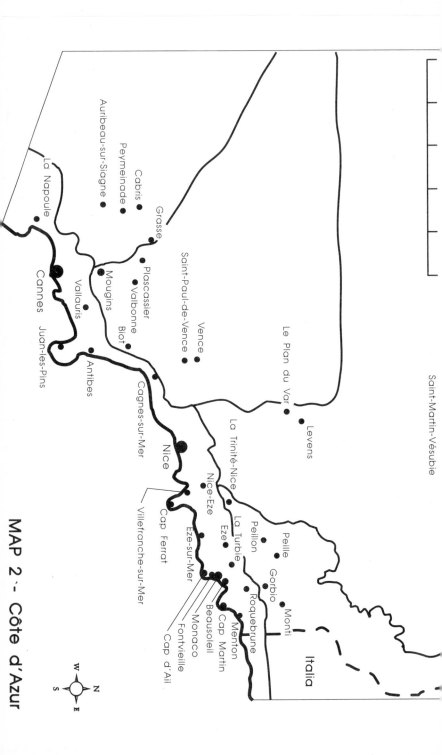

MAP 2 - Côte d'Azur

Chapter Eight
CANNNES AND ENVIRONS

The fertile coastal plain of this region was inhabited by Ligurians in pre-Roman times. These farmers protected themselves from invaders by building fortifications in the hills to which they would retreat at times of attack. The Greeks of Marseille then settled Nice as a trading post and the Romans, after colonising the area, expanded both Nice as a port, and the hill villages as look-out posts in visual contact with one another.

The Romans brought real peace to the region, and an exodus from the hills to the plains occurred. But the reversal quickly happened when the Roman Empire collapsed. The region then had a mixed history until the eighteenth century when Nice and then its surroundings came into fashion with the wealthy of northern countries who came in winter to enhance their health or recuperate from illness.

With the introduction of the railways in the nineteenth century the whole coastline quickly developed as a winter resort. The English were at the forefront of this invasion. Once having visited the region they returned to buy land, and built many fine homes, where they spent their winters. Around this time the name 'Côte d'Azur' became popular, and most visitors know the region by that name more than 'Alpes Maritimes', the official name of the *département*.

The hill villages remained cut off until the end of the last and beginning of this century when artists discovered these villages and found them far more attractive and less expensive. St Paul de Vence is such a case, discovered by artists and now very fashionable. As tourists rushed to the south in the summer months to bronze their pale bodies, more and more residents and tourists alike appreciated the climate yet wished for peace and quiet. Gradually they moved away from the beaches and into the hills. Where there had once been olive groves with shepherds grazing their flocks, estates of so-called *Mas Provençaux* sprang up to satisfy these new residential needs.

There are said to be over four thousand restaurants in Les Alpes Maritimes. I certainly have not counted them and certainly not visited them all. In the ensuing pages I am going to cover all the main towns of this famous area and direct you to restaurants both there and also off the beaten track. You will find many restaurants and cafés in the ports and on the beach fronts. Generally I have left these for you to try according to your taste and depth of pocket. Some are excellent but prices due to a special position and view are always higher than those found in streets further back.

Most of you will arrive on the Côte d'Azur either by plane to Nice airport, or along the *autoroute* from Aix and through the Department of the Var by car. Others will come south by train. Those of you who have chosen the train have most probably taken the best approach to this region. The railway came well before the car or plane. In fact it came before the people, who helped to make this area into a playground. The train having come first chose the best route along the sea from Fréjus. Either car or train will bring you first to:

LA NAPOULE

Here for many many years a restaurant called L'OASIS attracted everyone on the coast who wanted a great meal. The owner/chef retired and the place closed. Now it has just re-opened but as I have not yet eaten there I cannot point you in that direction. If by chance you find yourself in the port here or have arrived at lunch time you could do worse than eat at:

LA BROCHERIE II, Port de la Napoule

Tel: 93 49 80 73. Closed: Monday evening and Tuesday out of season. Fixed price menu: F175. M. Bonnin.

This restaurant is well positioned above the port with a warm welcoming interior decorated with nets and cork floats and accessories that go with the local fishermen. There is even flowing water with a pond containing *langouste* for you to choose and eat. The open-air terrace is well frequented in the summer and on good days out of season. Here you look down on the bustle of the port, one of my favourite pastimes. I find I can sit and watch the simple activities in a port all day. When I had a boat I found it just as soothing fiddling about on the boat and quay-side.

The fixed price menu is for four courses and I would suggest you choose from this, otherwise you will find this restaurant can be an expensive place to eat. If, for example you choose a main course of perhaps turbot and follow with a dessert the price would be about the same as the four courses on the fixed price menu. The food is very well prepared and presented. As you can imagine from the setting and décor, the majority of the dishes are fish, but there are good meat dishes for those who prefer it.

The wines are not a gift, priced at nearly 100 francs for a good Côtes de Provence and similar prices for wines from other well-known regions. A good dinner for two will come to around 500 francs if you both have the fixed price menu. The problem with this restaurant is they allow their position and view to dictate the prices. Do you blame them? No, of course not; you and I would do the same. I still go back as the food is good, but the position is even better.

Food: 7½   **Ambiance: 8½**   **Service: 6½**

At the other end of the Bay of La Napoule is the much more famous town of:

CANNES

Cannes was only a tiny fishing village until 1834. By chance Lord Brougham was travelling to Nice for his holidays and heard there was an epidemic of cholera there, so he alighted from the train at Cannes. He found it much more to his liking so duly bought a property and had a villa built. As he was Lord Chancellor, many ambitious people felt it would be advisable to follow suit, so Cannes promptly became very fashionable with the British.

Today it is a very well known centre for many conferences and festivals. The annual goings-on at the Film Festival are watched avidly by many million people all over the world. Conferences and of course holiday-makers have pushed Cannes to create hotels and restaurants of good quality to continue attracting this type of business.

Facing the town are two islands known as Les Iles de Lerins. On the nearer one, Ste Margarite, is a fort where supposedly the man in the iron mask was kept prisoner. The other is famous for a restaurant called Frédéric:

FREDERIC, Ile St Honorat

Tel: 93 48 66 88. Closed: October to Easter.

Here one can enjoy lobster done to their special recipe with onions. Yes! Most people would say the same as you – 'ONIONS . . . UGH'. But try it once and you will look forward to it the next time. I do not have a friend who has eaten there and would refuse an invitation to return. The setting is idyllic, under trees at the water's edge. In the summer heat it is wonderfully shaded and cool. It needs to be cool when you receive the bill, especially if you have all had lobster. Do not expect change from 500 francs each.

You may ask: 'How do we get across to the islands?'. Easy, there is a ferry that regularly goes from the port of Cannes, and it drops you a stone's throw from the restaurant. Whilst you are on the island there are a couple of things to see. First the ruined castle on the other side, and second a monastery belonging to a silent order.

At the latter you can stay for a few days and experience a retreat. The other way to get to the islands is to find a friend with a boat. The trip from Cannes or Golfe Juan is very short. You can anchor in front of the restaurant and call out – they will send out a tender to collect you.

Back to the mainland where we visit a restaurant that is well known and is literally translated as 'The Badly Seated'.

AU MAL ASSIS, Quai Saint-Pierre

Tel: 93 39 13 38. Closed: Mondays out of season.
Fixed price menus: F110 to F190. Robert and Noel.

The two owners inherited the business from their father, who had begun here, facing the port, in 1947. Robert's wife and Noel's son also work here. so it is really a family affair. The name, Noel told us, can be explained by either of two possibilities: that a tree from Malaysia ('*Malaysie*') was planted nearby; or from the old habit that the males used to sit in the bars or bistros and the females used to wait outside. The name could then have been shortened from '*male assis*' to '*mal assis*'. He said there were several bars and bistros with this name along the coast. This site has been a bistro since 1860. When his father started there were only 60 restaurants in and around Cannes; now there are nearly 200 in the town and at least 75 in the surrounding villages. The problem is that anyone can hire a chef and open a restaurant, even if they have no experience.

The interior of the restaurant is nothing special: very functional and a little old fashioned. I would not recommend you to go in mid-winter on a cold evening; then you want something cosy, maybe with a fire. On sunny days and from May to October the place operates on the pavement. Here they can seat well over one hundred, and despite the main road between it and the port there is always a great deal of activity which adds to the ambiance. You will find the fish fresh, the service good and attentive and the general atmosphere full of fun. The last time we went we started with an avocado and a *soupe de poisson*. They make and sell over 200 litres of this fish soup per day so you know it is fresh. We both had *loup de mer* (sea bass), served with boiled potatoes and a butter sauce. The fish was well seasoned with herbs and grilled to perfection. We both had dessert, which is rare as I often prefer cheese, but we chose a fruit salad and a fresh pineapple. I often enjoy the latter as it leaves your palate so clean and fresh. We had taken Noel's suggestion on the wine and drank the Estandon Numerote. I don't usually order Estandon as most of it is from a large *Coopérative*, but this was top of the range at 80 francs a bottle and not bad at all. A couple of coffees and a bottle of mineral water and the meal came to around 450 francs. Very good value, especially as we had had a good-size fish between the two of us.

If we had stuck to the fixed price menu we would have eaten very well for about a hundred francs less, but the *loup* was not on any of the set menus. If you want fish soup, there are not any places better than this in Cannes.

Food: 8   *Ambiance: 7½*   *Service: 8*

For something more cosy in the winter months go to the:

LE MESCLUN, 16 rue St. Antoine

Tel.: 93 99 45 19. Closed: Wednesdays. Fixed price menu: F170. Jean-Pierre Descoux and Dominique Guédon.

This can be found in a *rue piéton* (pedestrian district) near the main market opposite the old port. You can park in the old market or on its roof until midnight. This place was recommended to me by one of our listeners on the Radio Riviera open line. The names of the owners are difficult to pronounce, yet thank goodness they are very welcoming to the public who find their very attractively decorated place. Even though small, the room is broken up by having a mezzanine at the opposite end to the entrance. All the furnishings including the table-ware are of the highest quality.

The fixed price menu at 170 francs is surprisingly good value as the dishes are finely prepared, full of flavour and elegantly presented.

When I first saw the price of the set menu I felt it was too high but as we progressed through each plate I was more than satisfied it wasn't that expensive. If you aren't ready to enjoy an *amuse-gueule* and four courses the *à la carte* is a little pricey. I started with a *salade de béatilles et caille rôti*, different leaves served with slices of roast quail, the leaves tending to take away the stronger flavour of the meat. My main choice was *filet mignon de porc au miel poivré*. One doesn't get offered the fillet of pork very often; served with a honeyed pepper sauce this was absolutely delicious. The pepper-corns gave it bite yet the honey acted in the same way as traditional apple sauce, that is to take away any fatty flavour.

Cheese was again an interesting selection. I chose a cheese new to me: Sumatra. I thought it might have been foreign with a name like that, but no, just another example of the wide variety produced in France, this one from the region between Paris and Champagne, slightly closer to the latter. Dessert and coffee. The bill when it arrived just scraped under the five hundred for two. For the quality of food and presentation, not bad at all. As for the wine, we had drunk a Château Minuty, one of the better known Côtes de Provence brands, at 120 francs a bottle – a little high.

Another restaurant for those cold days is one you would not expect to find on the Côte d'Azur, since it is a typical Swiss place serving Swiss specialities. Not somewhere I would recommend to visitors, especially not in summer, but useful to those who live in the south permanently:

LA CANNASUISSE, 23 rue Forville

Tel: 93 99 01 27. Closed: Sundays. Fixed price menu: F120.
A Swiss lady and her twin daughters.

This is easily found as it is a couple of streets behind the market. The restaurant is actually housed in the vaulted cellars of the building. The dishes on offer are *viande de Grison*, *fondue*, *raclette* and grills which are prepared on the open fire. Wines also start at a reasonable level, with reds at F45/F35, whites and rosé at F55/F38. The wine list also includes other regions and of course some Swiss wines which I find pricey. Among the four of us, two chose the fixed price menu and the others ate *à la carte*. The dishes all had a Swiss flavour and with a bottle of wine and coffees the bill came to under 150 francs each all in.

Food: 7   *Ambiance: 7*   *Service: 7*

Although it is air conditioned when the weather is warm, I still feel this is best on cold winter evenings.

Cannes has about two hundred restaurants, many of them good quality but very pricey. Obviously Cannes is very fashionable. Its conventions such as MIDEM and the Film Festival bring in people with large expense accounts so the hotels and restaurants have generally hiked up their prices. In this town especially it pays to look at the menus posted in front before entering. I have often mentioned on my radio programme that I always think it is difficult to find a fantastic, good-value place here. Eventually one listener recommended:

LE JARDIN, 15 avenue Isola Bella

Tel.: 93 38 17 85. Closed: Sundays.
Fixed price menu: F65. M. Pitou.

Yes. believe it or not, 65 francs, for three courses which also includes a 25cl carafe of wine or a quarter bottle of mineral water. To find it is simple enough: find the boulevard de la République follow it north and the restaurant will be on your right a few streets up. The place itself is simple, with a long bar and tables inside, but a wonderfully sheltered sun-filled garden at the back.

The restaurant has *à la carte* but the fixed price *table d'hôte* has a large choice. For starters there are ten different dishes, including terrine, *moules marinières*, quiche, tomato and mozzarella cheese. I took the *salade Niçoise*. The main course also included a good choice, *filet de rascasse, faux filet, pavé aux échalotes* and two other dishes they change daily. That day there was *tripe à la Niçoise* or *sauté de veau*. I chose the lattér, which came with noodles. I chose the cheese instead of dessert though my neighbours had *crème caramel* and a vanilla ice cream. I sat and read my newspaper in the sun and sipped at my coffee. The other lunchers were all local and ate here regularly. I could see them wondering how this English person had found their secret hide-away. Secret no more. When I asked the patron his name, he replied that he was known as Monsieur Pitou, but that wasn't his real name. Go and enjoy it: three courses, wine, and coffee all for 71 francs. Beat that if you can in Cannes.

Food: 7½   **Ambiance:** 7½   **Service:** 7½

I must say I just love finding places like this. Thank you to my listener for phoning in.

Some of my other favourites in this town are:

VESUVIO, La Croisette

Tel: no reservations. Closed: hardly ever.

This offers Italian and French specialities. There is always a queue, even on a winter Saturday.

LE RAGTIME, 1 La Croisette

Tel: 93 68 47 10. Closed: Sundays out of season.

A place to go with a group, and for those who enjoy New Orleans ragtime. The food is much better than one normally finds in places such as these.

The best restaurants in Cannes are generally found in the best hotels, all on La Croisette, the famous sea-front, or a stone's throw away. These hotels have made great efforts in the last few years to match the quality of the restaurants in the nearby small village of Mougins. I list them in geographical order down the Croisette, rather than try to guess which one is best, as they are all so close in quality:

ROYAL GRAY, Hotel Gray d'Albion

Tel: 93 99 04 59. Closed: Monday dinner and Sundays.
Fixed price menus: F370 to F500. Jacques Chibois.

LA BELLE OTERO, Hotel Carlton

Tel: 93 39 69 69. Open: Dinner only.
Fixed price menu: F550. Francis Chauveau .

LA COTE, Hotel Carlton

Tel: 93 68 91 68. Closed: Tuesdays and Wednesdays.
Fixed price menu: F480. Sylvain Duparc.

LA PALME d'OR, Hotel Martinez

Tel: 92 98 30 18. Closed: Mondays and Tuesday lunch.
Fixed price menus: F280 to F480. Christian Willer.

In all the above I have listed the names of the restaurant chefs.

VALLAURIS

This town to the north-east of Cannes was a tiny village until after the last war. It always specialised in ceramics and Picasso worked on many of his ceramics here. Now it is full of little shops that sell local wares. The town has few eating places, let alone those worth mentioning. One I had heard of through someone who had sold me a couple of boats over the years. By chance, I was invited to dine by an acquaintance who worked for one of the other famous food guides. I was taken to the same restaurant Henry had always promised to take me to. Guess who was dining there the same evening? Yes, Henry and a couple of guests. The place is called:

LA GOUSSE d'AIL, 11, avenue de Grasse

Tel: 93 64 10 71. Closed: Tuesdays.
Fixed price menus: F105 to F200. M. Morato.

This is very much a country-style dining room, with stone walls and beamed ceilings. Another room has just been opened so one does not have to elbow one's way to the table any longer. The new room also has a fireplace which will be cosier in winter. The three set menus give everyone a good choice. The wines are also within everyone's pocket, starting at F35/F50 for the *vin de table*, with the Côtes de Provence starting at F45/F70. The wine list has a good choice of other regions, so all tastes can be satisfied. As we were there to gauge the restaurant for another guide, I took the advice to order the *Menu Gourmand* at 160 francs. I was instructed that most guides usually test a place on the middle or upper price menus. I usually measure a place on the lowest-priced one.

We ordered a Côtes de Provence: the rule is always to order the wine of the region. I usually do so as long as the restaurant has not hiked the price higher than that on better wines. The rosé wine arrived. We started with a *terrine de rascasse* and I had a dish of mussels and clams with garlic, prepared in the same way as snails. I had then chosen a *sole goujonette*, small pieces of sole cooked in a light batter. My expert friend took a *loup* with a hot butter sauce and lemon. It looked as good as my first course had tasted. We both chose a hot pear tart. Monsieur Morato is well known for for his desserts and this was light, not too sweet yet ever so slightly moist. Coffees and the bill arrived at 446 francs. My friend Henry had been right about his local: good quality and good value.

Food: 8 **Ambiance: 7½** **Service: 7½**

MOUGINS

Situated north of Cannes on the way to Grasse, this village has been inhabited since the stone age. Originally sited on the adjoining hill of Notre-Dame-de-Vie, it was moved to its present location for reasons of defence and security. Mougins then became a fortified Roman market city and if you look at it from a distance you can see clearly how it sits on the summit of the hill. The original Roman portal gate is still visible in the town.

After the Romans it became the property of the Comte d'Antibes who held it until the eleventh century, at which time he gave it to the Abbé de Lerins. It remained under the Abbé's control until the French Revolution. In the next two centuries Mougins suffered more than in the previous two millenniums. In the eighteenth century it was pillaged by the Austro-Sardinian armies and later in the same century it fell and was occupied by the Hungarians.

When you regard the views from Mougins itself you immediately realise the significance of its past history. To the south you can see Cannes and La Napoule on one side and the Isles of Lerins to the other. Westwards the Esterel mountains and the Tanneron, and north Grasse and the Alps. In this century the town was rebuilt and now the whole area is a fashionable residential centre. With the increase in value of property, shops began closing down and now very few remain. The most astonishing thing is how over the last 25 years more and more restaurants have opened. These are of excellent quality and now Mougins must have more first class eating establishments per inhabitant than any other town.

When you talk of food and Mougins in the same breath, you automatically think of the renowned chef Roger Vergé. He is the father of modern day restaurant cuisine in the South of France. He has two restaurants in the village and also his cooking school.

There is an abundance of places to eat here but sadly most of them, even though excellent, are pricey. The two that are good value are the Feu Follet and Le Bistrot de Mougins. Both are in the centre of the village. Of the two my favourite is:

FEU FOLLET, Place de la Mairie

Tel: 93 90 15 78. Closed: Sunday dinner and Mondays.
Fixed price menus: F135 and F160. Jean-Paul Battaglia.

To arrive at this restaurant you have to pass practically all the rest. Here you are next to the small but very attractive *Hôtel de Ville* (Town Hall). For years, as a child, I could not understand this and my father tried to make me see that *Hôtel* in old French stood for an individual large house or building standing on its own in town – in the way we refer to a 'hall' or a large mansion in the country.

Back to the Feu Follet, where Jean-Paul is hard at work preparing our meal. He comes from a restaurant tradition: his brother is the owner-chef of the Auberge Fleurie as you arrive at Valbonne; Micheline, his wife, is the daughter of André Surmain who has the Relais just opposite. Micheline, smiling a welcome, takes you to a table. Whether inside or out on the terrace, the tables are well placed. I love the terrace because you can watch all the passers-by near the village fountain. As a family we all enjoy this restaurant.

Both menus are for three courses, each has a choice of at least three dishes per course and you can take both cheese and dessert for a small supplement to the menu price. You can drink the house Côtes de Provence at F35/65 which is excellent. If you are going to drink local wine you need choose no other. I usually choose the lower price menu but have both the cheese and the dessert and still come out cheaper than the other menu which my daughters prefer as they love the *mousse au chocolat blanc*. Let us start at the beginning: my younger daughter, Victoria, had a *salade gourmande*, a dish my wife regularly chooses, while I opted for the *soupe de poisson*. My main course was a chicken with tarragon and Victoria had been imaginative and ordered the *cuisse d'agneau en croute*; lamb done like 'beef Wellington'. I have never seen this offered anywhere else. As I mentioned before, I took the cheese, which was a blue cheese served with a small salad. To end I had the *tarte paysanne* (that is what my daughter called me for not going for that white chocolate mousse). I find the mousse too sweet for me, but the tart with its very thin pastry and finely sliced apples I consider just right to finish a meal. As I was the only one to have a coffee we just scraped under 400 francs for a fabulous meal.

Micheline has a great team of youngsters to serve at table and you are always well attended to, yet never hurried. We have also been with a large group of friends in summer, both young and old, and sat outside until they are practically putting the chairs on the tables. One of our favourite restaurants on the coast. Go and try that chocolate mousse: I hope you have a sweet tooth.

Food: 8½   *Ambiance: 8½*   *Service: 8½*

Another place, a little different, in Mougins is a small hotel on the side facing Grasse, so really you have to go through the village to get to it. This is a lovely place to stay; maybe a little expensive but special. To eat there you must go for lunch as that is reasonable value for money.

MAS CANDILLE, boulevard Rebuffel

Tel: 93 90 00 85. Open: All year round.
Fixed price menus: F140 to F240. William Eve.

You really will be surprised when you arrive. It is an old *Mas* which has been extremely well converted into a small hotel, with a good dining room. The situation is enviable, quiet with a splendid view. You can sit on the terrace and enjoy the view as well as a very well prepared and well served meal. It is French cuisine ever-so-slightly anglicised.

The whole place is decorated with local antiques, so that when you are in the bar or the sitting room you feel miles from anywhere. So tranquil yet you are only a few hundred metres from Mougins village and only a few miles from Cannes and the sea.

Food: 8½   *Ambiance: 8½*   *Service: 8*

To list some of the other famous places in Mougins is a pleasure. I have eaten in eight different excellent restaurants in this town. I find them all good. Of course some are better for certain occasions than others. So when you choose be sure to work out why you are going to a particular place.

I was lucky to lunch one day with the great chef himself, Roger Vergé, who told me he was sad that many people now came to the Moulin to criticise and not enjoy. Such a shame. I must say I always go to enjoy myself every time I go out to eat.

A restaurant, whatever the standard, is there to serve you, the customers. Without you there is no business. In general the hotels and restaurants in the south of France have improved their standards, their quality, their service and their presentation enormously over the last ten years.

Here are some places of note:

MOULIN DE MOUGINS, Notre-Dame-de-Vie

Tel: 93 75 78 24. Closed: Monday and Thursday lunch.
Fixed price menu: F650. Roger Vergé.

FERME DE MOUGINS, St-Basile

Tel: 93 90 0374. Closed: Sunday dinner and Mondays.
Fixed price menus: F250 and F380. M. Sauvanet.

RELAIS A MOUGINS, place de la Mairie

Tel: 93 90 03 47. Closed: Mondays and Tuesday lunch.
Fixed price menus: F125 to F425. André Surmain.

LES MUSCADINS, 18 boulevard Courteline

Tel: 93 90 00 43. Closed: Wednesday lunch.
Fixed price menus: F200 and F320. Patricia Charrier.

L'AMANDIER DE MOUGINS, Place de Cdt-Lamy

Tel: 93 90 09 91. Closed: Wednesdays and Saturday lunch.
Fixed price menus: F220 (lunch only) and F330. Roger Vergé.

So that you can also try the Bistrot that I talked about at the beginning I list its details. It is in a seventeenth century stable built in stone. The two owners will give you a warm welcome:

BISTROT DE MOUGINS, place du Village

Tel: 93 75 78 34. Closed: Tuesdays and Wednesdays.
Fixed price menu: F150. A Ballatore and J-P Giordano.

As mentioned before, Mougins now has few shops. There are a few antique shops and a small shop run by Madame Vergé, in which she sells a variety of things edible and otherwise. There is also a lovely old village wash house that is now an art gallery.

GRASSE

The name of this medieval town supposedly originates from the Roman Consul 'Crassus'. By the twelfth century it was certainly a fortified city and by the seventeenth century was already well known for its flowers, scents, oils and soaps. It was also famous for its tanned hides, and from these two industries created a scented glove that was in great demand and remained fashionable for many hundred of years. Its situation, dominant over the plains that surround it, made it difficult to attack, and those very plains were the source of its wealth. They were covered with the famous mimosa, carnations, jasmine, roses and violets. The Grassois had also developed the way of mixing the distillation of the flowers with a spirit, that kept the perfume alive much longer. Today there are still many perfume manufacturers in Grasse as well as those that develop concentrates that form the basis of well-known brands.

The new town now dominates the old, but it is in the old town that you find charm and warmth. The town's most famous son was Fragonard the artist, but many great people came, stayed a while and went. These included Catherine de Medici, who on returning to Florence sent off a local perfumer to set up a distillery and learn the art of blending. Napoleon's sister Pauline lived here after the death of her husband Prince Borghese. Napoleon himself stayed on his return from Elba, hence the *route Napoléon*. Even Queen Victoria used to come and stay at the Grand Hotel.

One would think that with its history, its perfume and other industries Grasse would be a bustling town with good restaurants and hotels. Not at all. Most good restaurants are in the surrounding villages, and really there is no hotel of note, so that most people make the short journey to Cannes and stay there, since it is much more lively. The only restaurant worth noting is:

L'AMPHITRYON, 16 boulevard Victor-Hugo

Tel: 93 36 58 73. Closed: Sundays.
Fixed price menus: F108 to F225. M. Andre.

We then go quickly north several kilometres to the other side of Grasse to the charming village of:

CABRIS

LE PETIT PRINCE, 15 rue Frederic Mistral

Tel: 93 60 51 40. Closed: Thursday dinner and Fridays.
Fixed price menus: F98 to F188. Christian Massot.

Finding this restaurant was one of those lovely surprises one has only once or twice in a lifetime. It is not extraordinary, it is just exactly as you would want to find a welcoming place to eat. A traditional French restaurant with the people who run it of a 'certain age'. The setting, the service has that certain something. Not smart, not chic, just so.

But first a little history. *Le Petit Prince* is a well known book in France written by St Exupéry, a great aviator who completed the first flight from Dakaar to the USA. St Exupéry was also a well-known historian of aviation, a good poet and philosopher.

Cabris itself also has a romantic story. It was invaded and occupied by the Moors. When they were eventually driven out their leader threw a golden goat (*cabri*) into the nearby lake. People have been searching for it ever since. In fact, the village has been a meeting place for many artists and writers. It also had a Roman past as can still be seen by the antique washing troughs that were in use only a few years ago.

After we arrived at Le Petit Prince one of us had the 98 franc menu and the other the 138 franc one. Guess who had the latter? Yes, me of course. We ordered a bottle of Albergist, a secondary *appellation* of Domaine Ott, a strong red like a Cahors yet much more fruity and a little less tannic as well. The dishes we picked were very different to our normal choice. My guest had a melon, while I started with a *salade Carienne* – this included lettuce, tomatoes and slightly warm goat's cheese. I then had my extra course for which I had chosen a *mille feuille* pastry of smoked salmon, absolutely light and delicious. The main courses were a grilled steak and I had the *côte de porc au poivre*, much lighter than I expected. Cheese was offered but we declined, the desserts were too tempting. My guest seemed in need of the *tarte pruneaux noix de coco*, and duly demolished it without allowing me a taste. I was pleased to have the peaches in red wine that my wife rarely produces although she knows I so enjoy them. Maybe it dates from one of our first dinner parties just after we were married. When we got to the dessert course, peaches in red wine were placed on the table. All our friends had some and everyone accepted a second helping. I thought they were just exquisite, so I turned to my wife and asked what had she cooked them in. She answered that she had taken one of the bottles out of a wooden case. Unknowingly she had used a vintage bottle of Château La Tour for the cooking. That dinner all those years ago cost more than this one.

Madame Massot brought the coffees and I requested the bill. She and her staff had looked after us so well. Again and again I find in France so many restaurants produce great meals like this, for really very little. The bill came to just over 400 francs, great value.

Le Petit Prince is certainly one of my favourites. Pity it is so far from home base. If you are in the vicinity do go and meet Madame Massot. You will find her welcoming.

Food:8   *Ambiance: 8*   *Service: 8*

Nearby on the road back to the department of Var and in the direction of Draguignan is the village of:

PEYMEINADE

AUBERGE DU CHANTEGRILL, Val de Tignet

Tel: 93 66 12 33. Closed: Mondays in summer.
Fixed price menus: F85 to F210. Jean-Pierre and Yvette Rostain.

This restaurant is well out in the country and it is advisable to telephone in the winter to see if they are open. Jean-Pierre Rostain said if things were quiet he tended to take a few days off. But they do lovely country meals and at Christmas and New Year's Eve they do something special. He, his wife and a team of three serve in the dining room, and as it is quite large they can be rushed off their feet. The last time we arrived just after everyone else and had to wait a few minutes until there were spare menus for us to look at. So the place has a great following and don't be surprised if it is full.

The wine is reasonable, starting at F49/32 for his house wine. A Côtes de Provence begins at F40/62, so if you stick to one of the set menus and a local wine it can be a more than reasonable meal. The 85 franc menu is for three courses; you get four courses at 115F and 155 francs. The big set menu is five courses. We began with melon with port and frogs' legs, then chose leg of hare and fillet of lamb for the main course, followed by a large platter of cheeses. I declined dessert but my guest took the *filette de fraises*. With coffees it came to 392 francs in all. Really not bad at all.

Food: 7   **Ambiance: 7**   **Service: 7**

AURIBEAU-SUR-SIAGNE

On the road from Grasse to Pegomas you will come to a picturesque village perched on a hill. The surrounding slopes are steep. Sadly most of the trees on these slopes were burnt in the forest fires a few summers ago. Fire also destroyed several houses and the restaurant:

LA VIGNETTE HAUTE, route de Village

Tel: 93 42 20 01. Closed: Mondays and Tuesday lunch.
Fixed price menus: F220 to F400. Madame Revel.

This lovely old country house has been rebuilt exactly as it was, very rustic yet very comfortable, full of country antiques and in the evenings romantically lit by candle light. The prices in the evenings are higher than at lunch time. The main course really determines the price of your meal. The starters are a selection of hors-d'oeuvre with pâtés and crudités. A good cheese board is included and a variety of desserts.

One goes there for the very special ambiance. The restaurant itself is situated in the old stables, at the end of which is an enclosed area behind glass, that contains several farm animals and a donkey. On summer evenings the whole place, including the gardens, is illuminated by candlelight, a truly wonderful sight. The place isn't cheap, as one finds it costs about 400 francs per person, yet it is very different.

Food: 7½   **Ambiance: 9**   **Service: 7**

The tiny village is quickly visited. From the medieval gate to the other end is literally a few hundred metres. There is a thirteenth century church worth a visit. The view over the Tanneron valley is spectacular especially in winter when the mimosa is all in bloom, now mercifully growing back after the fires.

We go back to the other side of Mougins to a village my family all love. We lived in Valbonne for some time, and our first full year in France was passed wonderfully here. We experienced all the seasons and became part of truly local life, even though we were English.

VALBONNE

Valbonne was a medieval village, reconstructed in the fourteenth century, with straight streets and all those that crossed were at right angles, which is unique in the region. In the centre is the place des Arcades, which is bounded by thirteen Roman arches. The village has been well restored, but sadly the 250-year-old elms that filled the square suffered from disease in the mid-1980s and were cut down. The two Auberges above the arches date from the seventeenth century, and still offer very reasonable meals.

The Romans were in the area from the second century. Later, in the fifth century, the village became a centre for many chapels and monasteries. The Cistercian monks built the church and abbey at the close of the twelfth century. The records show that at that time the name was 'Valis Bona', meaning good valley. It is also recorded that St Roch spent some time here and his small chapel is at the edge of the village; his feast day is still celebrated on the 16th of August.

At the start of this century the villagers began to plant a table-grape called Servan. It was found that the neighbouring micro-climate allowed this grape to be conserved in harvest-fresh condition right through the winter. This is unique to Valbonne and the village has a grape festival on the last Sunday in January; they also celebrate St Blaise in the first Sunday in February. At this time all the desserts are made from the local fresh grape. People come from miles around to participate in these festivities. If you intend to be there make sure you book early if you want to have lunch in one of the local restaurants.

The village has a great variety of places to eat, maybe not as upmarket as those in Mougins yet very good and great value. We will take them in order of arrival from Mougins or Cannes. The first is on the right:

LE RELAIS DE LA VIGNETTE,
route de Cannes

Tel: 93 42 05 82. Closed: Tuesdays.
Fixed price menus: F98 to F170. M. Halibert.

The 98 franc menu is only available at lunch time in mid-week. The other times there are two menus: a four course menu at 120 francs and the 170 franc menu offering five courses. The wines, on the other hand, I find are not good value at all. A *vin de table* Pays des Maures is listed at 80 francs and the least expensive Côtes de Provence is 55/100 francs for a half-bottle or bottle,

We were a party of three and we all chose the 120 franc menu and each had something different for each course. As starters we had *gâteau de poisson,* a *raviolis frais* and a *terrine des légumes*. All very different, well presented and tasty. When this particular couple dine with me, he always chooses rabbit or hare; he didn't fail me this time, he had the rabbit. His wife chose the *roulade de poisson,* a roll of fish stuffed with herbs. I had the *confit cuisse de vollaille*. The cheese dish was very different, in that there was no choice, a brie sliced in half and stuffed with herbs and peppercorns which really livened up the taste of the brie. For dessert again we sampled a variety, one had the chocolate mousse, another a *crêpe Suzette* and I the *crème caramel*. We had two bottles of mineral water and three coffees. We had drunk a bottle of Sancerre at 160 francs – very expensive – yet when the bill arrived it was a reasonable 586 francs. Just under 200 francs each for four courses with wine, water and coffee.

The restaurant is owned by the same family that owns La Vignette Haute, in Auribeau. Here I find the food finer and of better quality, but the setting does not have the same charm. It is well decorated with wrought iron and impressive chairs, yet it doesn't have quite the same warmth. Still very good.

Food: 8   **Ambiance: 8**   *Service: 7½*

Just a little further on towards Valbonne but on the other side of the road is another good place to enjoy a meal. Here you find Jean-Pierre the brother of Jean-Paul of the Feu Follet in Mougins.

L'AUBERGE FLEURIE, route de Cannes

Tel: 93 42 02 80. Closed: Wednesdays.
Fixed price menus: F98 to F160. Jean-Pierre Battaglia.

Both brothers seem to structure their menus in similar fashion. Here at the Auberge Fleurie prices are a little more reasonable. I suppose all prices in Mougins restaurants are higher and the Feu Follet deserves to get away with a higher price as well. The thing that pleases me here is that the wines are so reasonable. You can have a *pichet*, equivalent in size to a bottle, for as little as 25 francs and the half bottle equivalent for 15 francs. His other wines are just as competitive, Château La Coste from near Aix 35/55F, a Loire wine at 65F and a Beaujolais at 75 francs. The rest of the wine list is equivalently priced.

There are three menus: three courses at 98 francs and 130 francs, and four courses at 160 francs. Another nice touch; while you are choosing what you are going to order they place olives and crispy snacks on the table. We were four, my three guests were a couple who had bought a boat from me and their daughter. He chose the 98 franc menu and the three of us had the 130 franc menu.

There are two parts to the restaurant, the original room in the auberge and the covered terrace. Each section holds about sixty, but as the place is very popular it fills up even in the off season, so do book otherwise you could be disappointed. That particular evening the place was practically full when we arrived, a real buzz throughout the dining room, which always helps the atmosphere.

The special dishes of the day were *quenelles* of trout and clams for starters, poached mixed fish as the main course and fresh strawberries with a strawberry sauce and ice cream for dessert.

The choice from the 98 franc menu was impressive; *soupe de pêcheur* then *lapin à la graine de moutarde* and my guest finished with the strawberries. The rest of us didn't do so badly, two had *quenelles* and I had the *salade gourmande*. Then *magret de canard* for one, *saumon au gros sel* for my other guest and *cuisse de volaille* for me. All excellent, especially the salmon done in a shell of sea salt. For desserts my friends' daughter had the *pavé au chocolat*, a lethal chunk of very rich chocolate cake; how does she keep so slim? Her mother had a *crème brulée* – and she is even thinner! And I on strawberries; the minute I look at food on goes the weight. We had enjoyed a bottle of Château La Coste at 55 francs. We ordered coffees and when they arrived so did a dish of chocolates. Of course the ladies ate them, not us, but it gives a lovely finishing touch. The bill for the four came to 625 francs and that included a couple of bottles of mineral water.

Food: 8   **Ambiance: 7½**   **Service: 7½**

If you try this Auberge and the Feu Follet in Mougins it is interesting to compare them. In both the quality of the food is good yet the latter is a little more sophisticated, which is why you end up paying a little more.

LA CAVE SAINT-BERNARDIN,
rue des Arcades

Tel: 93 42 03 88. Closed: Sundays and Mondays.
Fixed price menus: F120 and F150. Marie Jan and Jacques.

This is such a cute little restaurant just off the central square of the old village. You open the front door and you are right in the restaurant. There are two rooms that in total seat about thirty.

My wife and younger daughter had the 120 franc menu. Both of them started with a dozen snails each, very fleshy and with not more than a touch of garlic. I had home-made lasagne, the fine pasta leaves interleaved with a thick sauce and cheese. To follow, my wife had grilled scampi my daughter an *escalope de veau* and I a *truite meunière*. A large dish of several vegetables was placed on the table for us to help ourselves. A cheese tray to choose from and then dessert and coffees. During the meal we had drunk a bottle of Roquefeuillet rosé. You will find this Côtes de Provence on many wine lists here in the south, the reason being that this particular vineyard works very hard promoting its wines by offering the *restaurateur* a rebate at the end of the year related to the quantity they sell. This rebate is not paid as money but in work that needs to be done to the place, like new sun blinds.

We had chosen the wine from a list that started reasonably at 25/50 francs for the *réserve du restaurant*, and the rosé we chose was 76 francs a bottle.

The ever-attentive Marie brought the bill that came to 460 francs for the three of us for a four course meal. Again a reasonable place.

Food: 8   *Ambiance: 8*   *Service: 7*

Another good place here is in the new development opposite the post office:

LA TERRASSE, opposite Post Office

Tel: 93 40 25 00. Closed: Tuesdays.
Fixed price menus: F75 and F100. Charlie.

The 75 franc menu is available only at lunch time. Both menus are for three courses. The wine list is also reasonable, starting at 25/45 francs a bottle for a Côtes de Provence AOC, another at 30/47 francs and then upwards. All the wines are at fair prices. We visited on a cool evening last winter when it had just opened. Although clean and well decorated, because it was all new it looked a little cold and stark. In mid-summer we would have been thrilled with its cool appearance. There are lovely pictures of yesteryear Valbonne around the place, and it is fascinating to see how the village has evolved. A table on the mezzanine balcony floor must be popular when the place is full – a chance to survey the whole scene.

We both chose the 100 franc menu and had the *soupe de poisson* which arrived with all its trimmings, toast, garlic *rouille* and grated cheese. You put the *rouille* on the toast, sprinkle with grated cheese and float them, like small boats, on the top of the soup. It is almost a meal in itself. I had a grilled steak to follow served with an assortment of vegetables. From the small selection on the cheese-board I chose a cow's milk cream cheese. I could have chosen a dessert if I had preferred. We had coffees. The bill with the wine and a bottle of Badoit came to 285 francs. I think that is very fair.

Food 7½   *Ambiance: 7*   *Service: 7½*

This little place is owned by a gentleman called Charlie. He formerly had a simple restaurant in the village and due to the redevelopment he had to close down. This one he now operates with his daughter Mireille, and the chef is her boy-friend Philippe. Now you have the full story.

The two other places of note in the village are:

MOULIN DES MOINES, place Eglise

Tel: 93 42 03 41. Closed: Saturday and Monday lunch.
Fixed price menus: F95 to F180. Anick Rousseau.

BISTRO DE VALBONNE, rue Fountaine

Tel: 93 42 05 59. Closed: Sundays and Mondays.
Fixed price menus: F145 to F230.

Just up from Valbonne on the road to Grasse you come to:

PLASCASSIER

AUBERGE ST-DONAT or Chez Robert, at the crossroads

Tel: 93 60 10 07. Closed: every evening.
Fixed price menus: F58 and F100. Jean-Pierre Mariani.

Very easy: four courses for 58 francs in the week and 100 francs for six courses on Sundays. These prices include half a carafe of wine and coffee. The only problem is that there is no choice on the menu. I put this to our waiter: no problem was his reply, we can do a steak or omelette or something else. That day we were three and we all had a salad that contained endives, tomatoes, ham and croûtons. The second course was a real surprise: kidneys in small slices with a slightly mustard sauce. We swallowed the kidneys and mopped up the sauce with our bread. The main course contained two large lamb chops garnished with *pommes frites* and courgettes that had been tossed in scrambled eggs, very different indeed. For dessert there was a choice of fruit salad, chocolate mousse or *crème caramel*, as usual on practically every restaurant dessert list.

Never mind. The bill arrived and every one reached to pay for this treat, 174 francs for the three of us. Is that good value or not? I say astounding and unbelievable, but I was there and I testify that was the amount. They say the Sunday feast keeps you going all week. I must try it one day soon. It must be the best value restaurant on the Côte d'Azur

Food: 7   *Ambiance: 7½*   *Service: 7½*

The other place worth mentioning in Plascassier (but please don't even try and think it is as inexpensive as Chez Robert) is:

RELAIS DE SARTOUX, route de Valbonne

Tel: 93 60 10 57. Closed: Wednesdays.
Fixed price menus: F115 and F160.

Chapter Nine
ANTIBES TO VENCE

BIOT

This town was first occupied nearly two hundred years before Christ, and much of the Roman walls and portal gates remain in good order. It next came into prominence when the Count of Provence gave the Knights Templars rights over the land in 1209. These of course were the famous Knights of Malta. They abused their privileges and caused an uprising, until they and the Bishop of Antibes were finally put into prison in 1309. In the fourteenth century between the plague and invasions, the town was destroyed and remained desolate until the Bishop of Grasse brought in four dozen Genoese families to rebuild it in 1460. They started the ceramic and glass blowing that Biot is still famous for. To this day it is the home and workshop of many artists. You will enjoy wandering through the narrow streets looking at the different varieties of glass and ceramics. With the tourist invasion the inevitable small restaurants have sprung up but some are now of good standard and others are of reasonable value.

LE PLAT D'ETAIN, 20 rue St Sebastien

Tel: 93 65 09 37. Closed: Sunday dinner and Mondays.
Fixed price menus: F145 and F205. M. Angaud.

A small, well-decorated place with tables of different shapes and sizes which immediately makes the place more welcoming than one where the tables are all uniform. We were looked after by the owner and one assistant and since the place is small this was done with no difficulty. The owner told us he was from Gascony in south-west France, which is certainly well reputed for its food, so we looked forward to our meal.

The five of us were seated at an oval table that could easily have taken six and all chose the 130 franc menu. The wines were on the pricey side starting at 55/88 francs for a Côtes de Provence. I am always amazed in this part of France that restaurants produce good fixed price menus where a lot of work and thought goes into producing the dishes, but they add such huge margins to the wine that they buy and stock. We did in fact drink two bottles of red and one of white. Am I glad I am a guest this time!

The starters that were chosen were *fleurs de courgette*, *mousse de poisson* and *coeur de cerfeuil* (chervil). The stuffed courgettes flowers were wonderful and the chervil salad was something I had never had before and I was pleased to try it – very good indeed. For our main courses we chose a larger variety: a *pièce de boeuf au raisins*, one had *lotte*, another salmon and two had the *lapereau* (hare) with wild mushrooms and fresh pasta. The pasta is to take away any fat. I always find it may take it from the hare but adds it to my waistline. For dessert there was the usual selection plus another new dish to me, a tart of ginger, a very different flavour to finish with. We all agreed that the dishes were all beautifully presented and each felt they had eaten a well-balanced meal. The latter is so important.

My friends were from London and in advertising so when they got the bill, 1049 francs for the five of us, they laughed. 'We often spend this amount per person in London and think nothing of it' they told me. And here am I always complaining if I don't get a fantastic meal for under 250 francs. But I do think London has gone mad with its prices. Even in Paris which is the capital of food, you can still find many superb places offering wonderful meals and great atmosphere at reasonable prices.

Food: 8   *Ambiance: 7½*   *Service: 7½*

CAFE DE LA POSTE, 24 rue St Sebastien

Tel: 93 65 19 32. Closed: varies with the season.
Fixed price menu: none ,only à la carte. Jean-Paul Secchi.

I do hate places where they don't have fixed price menus. I quickly complained to Jean-Paul who said he felt I was right and he was in the process of correcting it. This is a restaurant I have been to off and on for many years. so when I heard it had a new owner I felt tempted to try it.

Starters ranged from F40 to 75 francs, and main courses from F60 to 98 francs, desserts from F30 to 90 francs. If you take the spread, that amounts to 130 to 263 francs if you have the three courses. On the other hand wines were fair, a Côtes de Provence AOC was 40/65 francs, Côtes du Rhône 50/80 francs and the wine list had a good selection from other regions. I chose the Château La Coste at 85 francs – not cheap, but we drank two bottles between the three of us.

The lady in the party had *omelette bistrot, mignon de veau à la crème et champignon de bois*, and a *tarte au citron* for dessert. My other guest started with *moules farcies* then *cassoulet au confit d'oie et sa saucisse de Toulouse* and a vanilla ice cream as dessert. For me a smoked salmon in filo pastry, then lamb in the provençal style, that is with tomatoes and garlic, and the *pièce de résistance* for dessert the *gâteau framboise*. This was the dish at 90 francs. Was it rich, but was it delicious! It had that tiny sharpness of raspberries, and it was as light as a feather. We got the bill as we drank a second coffee with the compliments of the owner. The damage was just over 750 francs, 250 francs each, the limit I had set myself.

Food: 8   *Ambiance: 8*   *Service: 6½*

Two other places of note in Biot. I have eaten in both but they are both above the maximum price limit I like to set myself:

AUBERGE DU JARRIER,
passage de la Bourgade

Tel: 93 65 11 68. Closed: Tuesday and Wednesday lunch.
Fixed price menus: F190 to F320 francs. M. Metral.

LES TERRAILLERS, route du Chemin-Neuf

Tel: 93 65 01 59. Closed: Wednesday and Thursday lunch.
Fixed price menus: F160 to F340. Messrs Fulci and Jacques.

JUAN-LES-PINS

Pass through here in winter and you can't believe it when you come back in summer; and vice versa. October arrives and everything shuts down; the shops become empty shells. At Easter a few businesses start re-opening but it takes until Whitsun for things to get into full swing. In summer it is a centre for every age group, full of noise and bustle and the town hardly sleeps for the next few months. I know my own children have loved it since they were eight to ten years old. The owners of the boutiques and shops are here in summer but in winter they are in one of the fashionable ski resorts.

There are many restaurants, but most are in the semi-fast food business. There are some very good places as well but these will be listed a little further on. As it isn't my habit to eat French cuisine in this environment, I usually have either something approaching Italian or something else in the same vein, so I am going to recommend somewhere that is a cross of Malay, Vietnamese and Thai:

LE POUSSE-POUSSE,
12 rue du Docteur Dautheville

Tel: 93 61 41 99. Closed: November to mid-February.
Fixed price menu: F85. Liza and Maurice.

Liza is Welsh and came to the south of France about sixteen years ago. She opened a shoe shop opposite. She met Maurice, from Marseille of Vietnamese origin, a few years ago, and they opened this restaurant together. It has been very successful and now they have another place in Antibes. I was first brought here by some good friends, Ron and Liz, who have a home between Valbonne and Biot. They have often been out with me searching for somewhere different, and this is their local. You won't be disappointed if you want to eat something oriental for a change while on holiday.

There are two menus at 85 francs, each is three courses, one is vegetarian. I was surprised to learn from Liza that three-quarters of Americans who eat there, always eat vegetarian. There is a wine list which starts at 85F for a Beaujolais, a Bordeaux at 50/90F and the Côtes de Provence 55/95 francs. I will say no more as you must realise how I feel with regard to wine prices. My host chose a Pinot Noir rosé at 150 francs. I asked him if he was putting out the boat that particular evening.

We took the advice of our hosts and did not order the fixed price menu, but all ordered from the *à la carte*. Ron had the Saigon soup, my wife the chicken Satay, Liz and I the Spring rolls that we had seen served at the next table. We had chosen well. I must say I was worried about soup in summer, as we were in the last week of June, but then my host ordered a *marmite Thailandaise*, a Siamese equivalent of *bouillabaisse*. His wife chose beef in perfumed mushrooms. My wife had the prawns with ginger and I chose chicken Pekinese style which is slightly hot and spicy. Three teas and a coffee, plus four digestives (a strong liqueur to help the meal go down). All in all a good meal for 824 francs. We sat on the pavement watching the throngs go back and forth, being served by two lovely young ladies, one a Vietnamese, the other the niece of the owner, one quarter Vietnamese, three-quarters French.

Food: 7   *Ambiance: 8*   *Service: 7*

The restaurant has two good things going for it; first, it serves good food, second, it is on a street where everyone strolls by to see and be seen. We had a marvellous evening looking at some of the beautiful people strutting along this street, either showing off their partners or themselves . . . GREAT FUN.

Juan-les-Pins has two very good restaurants:

LA TERRASSE, La Pinède

Tel: 93 61 20 37. Closed: lunch times and November to April.
Fixed price menu: F380 to F550. Christian Morisset.

BELLES RIVES, boulevard du Littoral

Tel: 93 61 02 79. Closed: September to Whitsun.
Fixed price menus: F280 to F480. M. Estene.

The former has developed some marvellous chefs, including Alain Ducasse, now at the Louis XV in Monaco where he has been awarded three stars. The latter is one of the nicest places on the whole Côte d'Azur to have lunch at the water's edge.

ANTIBES

In the fourth century BC the Greeks of Marseille created Antipolis as a trading post along the coast from Nice. The new, very successful, industrial park, Sophia Antipolis, got its name from Antibes' origins. The town has played a large role in the history of this region. Today it is the largest port on the Côte d'Azur and now contains two thousand pleasure craft. Only a couple of hundred years ago Napoleon defended the Mediterranean from here, and then the port was full of French battleships. Antibes, more than any other port on this coast, has remained as it was in Napoleon's time. If you enter old Antibes through the arches at the edge of the port, park your car on the sea wall, and stroll through the tiny streets, you will sense its seafaring past.

Here Napoleon landed after escaping from Elba. It was here that he made preparations for his return to Paris, taking the back route via Grasse and Grenoble. Sadly he suffered from indigestion so he couldn't have joined us on our visit to:

LE ROMARIN, 28 boulevard Mal-Leclerc

Tel: 93 61 54 29. Closed: Wednesdays.
Fixed price menus: F105 and F130. M. and Mme Boer.

This restaurant is on the sea-front but also at a roundabout at the western edge of the town. You can park outside, and keep an eye on the car. The restaurant has a small terrace and the interior has beams and is warmly decorated. The fish is fresh, the prices reasonable and you won't be disappointed with your meal. Madame looks after you quite well even though sometimes she pretends to be gruff.

The last time my wife and I lunched there, four French people at the next table were discussing their following Friday dinner. They told us they often came to this restaurant during their holidays, and always on the last Friday of their stay they came for the *bourride*, followed by a large fish and Monsieur's special tart. We had enjoyed the set 105 franc menu, and with a half bottle of wine and coffees it had come to 260 francs. We have never eaten dinner here but I understand the restaurant is always very full with regulars.

Food: 7½   *Ambiance: 7½*   *Service: 7½*

Another place we frequently go to is literally across the road from the market. We book and usually arrive at 12.45 pm. The reason for this is that the market becomes a car park after it closes at noon. Park your car and you are at the restaurant:

DU MATIN, 16 cours Massena

Tel: 93 34 23 10. Closed: Sundays.
Fixed price menus: F75 and F95. Christian and Véronique.

The cheaper menu is for two courses and the other for three courses. This tiny restaurant is hewn out of the rock and must have been a fishermen's store in centuries gone by. It seats about 24 inside and ten outside on the pavement. The wine is reasonable as well; you can order the house reserve at 35/50 francs for a half bottle or bottle.

The set menu is good and you can order a dish from the *à la carte* at a small surcharge. We had *coquille de fruits de mer* and a *brochette de scampis* (this had a 15 francs surcharge). Then we had *côte d'agneau* and my wife's favourite, their *tarte au citron* with finely sliced lemons. We had coffees and a mineral water and half a bottle of the Reserve; in all 275 francs. Honest fare and good portions. The place is simple, with no trimmings.

Food: **7**   *Ambiance:* **7**   *Service:* **7**

The best restaurant of Antibes is just outside the town on the old route Nationale N 7, in a large building standing on its own. Unfortunately on the other side of the road is the old railway.

LA BONNE AUBERGE, route N 7

Tel: 93 33 36 65. Closed: Mondays.
Fixed price menus: F370 to F570. Jo and Philippe Rostang.

I visited this restaurant for dinner with my first collaborator for my radio programme for Radio Riviera. This is a restaurant of long standing. Father Jo created it and ran it for many years, followed by his son Philippe, who has now taken over as chef. Any of us would be proud to have his CV. He passed out of hotelier college, then served apprenticeships under Senderens, the brothers Troisgros, Delaveyne and Maitre in Berlin. With all this behind him you would expect him to be much more than his thirty years. There is also another son, Michel, who has his own restaurant in Paris. They are certainly keeping it in the family.

The director of the restaurant is Jacques who runs a very able team who look after you with kid gloves. Jean-Jacques, the *sommelier*, offers a gentle guiding hand with your choice of wine. As you can imagine the wine list is impressive. You can't drink a *vin de table* with this sort of feast. For most of us, eating here has to be a special occasion. Even if you go for the cheapest menu and an inexpensive wine, you are talking of spending over 900 francs.

I will just run through the dishes, or should I call them master-pieces. Lucien had *rouget à la provençal, fleurs de courgettes, loup de mer,* grapefruit sorbet to clear the palate, pigeon, cheese (a chèvre and a slice of Pont-Evêque from Normandy) and *soufflé citron chocolat.* Does that make your mouth water? My menu was every bit as impressive. Salmon parcels with asparagus, lobster soup, *dorade,* prawns with polenta wrapped in spinach leaves, grapefruit sorbet, pink lamb lightly cooked, served with small tomatoes filled with wild rice, cheese (St Marcellin and Livarot) and rhubarb done with a *crème brulée.* A culinary voyage of beauty: fine tastes and a gentle touch . . . and of course ending with an empty pocket.

As it was late Philippe came and offered us a glass of Beaume de Venise, a dessert wine from near Orange in Vaucluse. He sat with us as we sipped the wine and drank a couple of coffees. The rest of the staff never made us feel it was time to go. The whole meal was very well served and presented; the way the plates are removed and the next set of cutlery is placed before you: it is all made to look so easy. Before leaving I asked if I could have a glance at the kitchen. It was bigger than I imagined, also spotless; all the copper pans were shiny and hanging in place; a true artist's operating room.

Food: 9½   **Ambiance: 8**½   **Service: 9**

Nearby there is Cap-d'Antibes where you will find the famous Eden Roc – the cliff top restaurant of the Grand Hotel du Cap where celebrities tend to stay. This past winter it was Madonna with her entourage. In the *belle époque* it was filled with monarchs and princes. How things have changed.

EDEN ROC, boulevard Kennedy

Tel: 93 61 39 01. Closed: end October to end March.
No fixed price menu but more than 650 francs. M. Irondelle.

RESTAURANT DE BACON,
boulevard de Bacon

Tel: 93 61 50 02. Closed: Sunday dinner and Mondays.
Fixed price menus: F350 and F450. Etienne Sordello.

CAGNES-SUR-MER

The old village of Haut-de-Cagnes was constructed by the Romans as a fortress to protect their route from Rome to Spain. It was first used by Caesar and later by the Crusaders. The present ramparts were built in the twelfth century and the château a hundred years later. In 1309 Robert of Anjou gave it to Rainier Grimaldi, at that time an admiral of France and the sovereign of Monaco. He rebuilt the château and much of this remains today. The Grimaldis remained lords of Cagnes until the French Revolution when the inhabitants pillaged the castle and the family took refuge in Nice. It was sold in 1875 for eight thousand francs to a private buyer. Eventually the town purchased it in 1937 and it now acts as a museum.

Many painters came to live here, including Renoir, whose house is now also a museum. The main local feast-day is that of Saint Jean on the 24th of June when folk dances take place and the whole hillside is lit up.

In nearby Villeneuve-Loubet a more important event took place, at least for those of us interested in good food. Here, behind the Mairie, Auguste Escoffier was born in 1847. His house is now a museum devoted to food, with a collection of fifteen thousand menus since 1820. At the height of his career he was the famous chef at the Carlton in London. It was he who created *Pêche Melba* for the great opera star, Madame Melba. When she put on too much weight he created light Melba Toast for her as well.

My favourite restaurant in Cagnes-sur-Mer is called:

LE PICADERO, 3 boulevard de la Plage

Tel: 93 73 57 81. Closed: Mondays.
Fixed price menus: F170 and F280. Vincent Miraglio.

My wife and I have been going to eat Vincent Miraglio's cooking since he first opened. This thirty-year-old, thin yet smiling chef did his training under Maximin at the Negresco in Nice and Ducasse at the Terrasse in Juan-les-Pins. His meals are delicately prepared dishes with a flavour and taste of the south of France. We are never disappointed with a meal whenever we go there. He has now opened a Bistro next door where the dishes are a little less pricey, yet come out of the same kitchen.

Last time we visited we were a party of three and each of us chose something different. We started with *salade tiède de rouget* (red mullet), *salade d'aiguillette de canard* and a *soupe d'homard*. Our main courses were even more impressive. *Le croustillant de loup de pays jus court au basilic, le blanc de palangre en sauce vin blanc,* and *leminée de boeuf jus au vin rouge.* For dessert *fromage de chèvre frais au basilic, le feuillantine aux pommes caramelisées* and *feuillette aux fruits rouges.* Just look at the variety of the dishes! The vegetables that come with the main course are also exquisitely prepared and dressed. All this out of a small kitchen with very little help.

Generally we find the restaurant is full of French people and often you find some of them are people who have their own restaurant enjoying their day off. A great, imaginative meal that with all the wine, water, etc. came to 250 francs per person.

Food: 9   *Ambiance: 8*   *Service: 8*

If you like horse racing the Hippodrome is very close to the Picadero. Here you can watch the racing and have a fabulous meal. The four course menu is 190 francs and the tables are terraced so all can watch the horses and enjoy a great lunch at the same time. We often go with a group of friends on a Sunday, especially in February and March when they have the flat races. There are usually trotters on the same race card. The service is done by a number of ladies of a certain age, and others come to take your bets and return you your winnings, if you are lucky.

Near the château there is a restaurant that other guides rate as the best in Cagnes:

LE CAGNARD, rue du Pontis-Long

Tel: 93 20 73 21. Closed: Thursday lunch.
Fixed price menus: F370 and F490. Félix and Mauricette Barel.

This fourteenth century house is one of the loveliest settings for a hotel and restaurant. One can't judge which is better, the interior or the view of the whole coast.

Another restaurant up in the old town is:

DES PEINTRES, 71 montée de la Bourgade

Tel: 93 20 83 08. Closed: Wednesdays.
Fixed price menus: F120 and F165. Jacques Lorquet.

This is found by following the one-way system all the way up to the castle. Park here, as on the way down it is difficult. Now follow the one way down for about two hundred metres. Jacques is the chef/patron and has named his menus after Modigliani and Breughel. Both menus are three courses but the wines are even better value. The house red or rosé and the blanc de blanc are 40/55 francs. The house red, a Côtes du Rhône-Villages, was tasty and not at all tannic.

The place has that fresh, Provençal look, dark-coloured beams with white walls. Paintings hang on the walls and there are antique and farmhouse objects here and there. The restaurant boasts a spectacular view over the roof-tops of Cagnes to the sea. The roof tiles are that very special shade of red, yellow and orange. Choose a reasonable local wine and you get a good value meal; if on the other hand you go for an expensive Chablis the bill may hurt.

Food 7½   *Ambiance: 8½*   *Service: 7*

Back down to Cagnes-ville and here you can have that different meal in the:

DOUCHKA, 19 avenue Renoir

Tel: 93 20 61 75. Closed: lunch times.
Fixed price menus: F130 and F160. Alain and Jocelyne.

I can't remember who took me to this fascinating place. It was just such a surprise when we walked in and there you were in the centre of Cagnes-sur-Mer but really somewhere outside Moscow. In fact, it is Russian with a very French touch. The two owners coped with all the service but there was also someone else who played Russian songs on demand.

The food is fun and I would suggest you choose ethnic food and stick to the menu. Go with a group and sing and make a noise. The only complaint was that the two owners spent so much time chatting to all of us, as if they ran the restaurant solely for that purpose. Good fun and you will come out for under 250 francs, especially if you stick to the fixed price menus.

Food: 7½ **Ambiance: 8** **Service: 6**

Another little place, this time on the coast, I visited with my Canadian godson. He chose the 190 franc menu and I went for the 120 franc menu.

L'AUBERGE DU PORT, boulevard de la Plage

Tel: 93 07 25 28. Closed: Wednesdays.
Fixed price menus: F120 and F190. Taine and Riri.

The two owners are actually fishermen. There is a terrace and in bad weather you can eat inside where all the cooking is done on the open fire. The wine list starts at a reasonable 30/55 francs a half bottle and bottle for a Coteaux Varois. We chose the house rosé which we found to be very good. My meal was three courses, *salade Niçoise*, then a *sole meunière* and then a *tarte au pomme avec glace vanille*. My godson, even though he has a good appetite, could not get through the larger menu with ease. This included *soupe de poisson*, *raviolis Niçoise*, *faux-filet et frites*, *salade*, *fromage* and a *mousse au chocolat*, his favourite. With coffees it came to 385 francs for the two of us. This was a cheap price to pay for a *grande bouffe* that would set him up for the week.

Food: **7**   *Ambiance:* **7**   *Service:* **7**

From Cagnes one takes the road to Vence and St Paul. These two places have an old history.

VENCE

The old city is still within the medieval walls and entry is by the Roman portal gates. The town was several times destroyed by the Lombards and Saracens. Once the latter were driven out in the ninth century the town truly prospered. Today it is a busy country town and you need to spend time there to get below the surface and sense its vitality. There are many fountains and the streets and squares are very picturesque. Our favourite restaurant here is:

AUBERGE DES SEIGNEURS, place Frene

Tel: 93 58 04 24. Closed: Sunday dinner and Mondays.
Fixed price menus: F160 and F180. Pierre Rodi.

This is indeed an old Provençal Auberge with five rooms. The old stone wash basin is just outside the toilets in the basement. The dining room is the old kitchen with an open fire where Monsieur Rodi cooks the main meat dishes. Most of the meat is roasted on a spit. There are lovely copper utensils hanging on the walls, the tables and chairs are in heavy wood, and in front of the fire is a huge thick table. This, Monsieur Rodi was quick to point out, was the table the King, Francois Premier, ate at on his visit to Vence. You know from the twinkle in his eye that it isn't all true. He goes on to tell us that the king shared this house with his mistress. In fact the king had come to Vence with the Archbishop Claud Farnese of Les Iles des Lerins. This Archbishop eventually became

Pope Paul III and was the person who built the Sistine Chapel. Food and all this history as well!

I advise you to have the fixed price menu and choose the *carré d'agneau*, done slightly pink. This is after the pâtés as starters and a *truite au bleu* as the fish course. The *tarte Tatin* is second only to that produced by my wife; this is the judgement of my children. The wine was reasonable and with coffee Monsieur brings a large bottle and offers you a glass of his *eau de vie*. In fact last time he filled my coffee cup, and he tells us it is made from 'love flowers'. He is such a lovely fellow! I suppose he should be retired, but he so adores looking after his customers.

Food: 8   *Ambiance: 9*   *Service: 7½*

For very good value there is:

LA FARIGOULE, 15 rue H-Isnard

Tel: 93 58 01 27. Closed: Friday and Saturday lunch.
Fixed price menus: F100 to F130. Georgette Castaud.

For the spectacular:

CHÂTEAU SAINT-MARTIN,
route de Coursegoules

Tel: 93 58 02 02. Closed: Wednesdays.
Fixed price menus: F300 to F450. Mlle Brunet.

A lovely old château in 34 acres of garden, furnished with antiques. The terrace where you have your meals has a vista to Nice airport and beyond.

Another place worth a visit is in the direction of Grasse:

CHATEAU DES AROMES, route de Grasse

Tel: 93 58 70 24. Closed: Sunday evening and Mondays.
Fixed price menus: F150 and F320. Luby and Geéard Mosinak.

Luby is English and Gérard comes from Béthune in the Pas de Calais. He ran a restaurant in London that was highly rated. Here he is his own boss having leased the restaurant from the owners of the château.

The château itself is a lovely setting for a restaurant especially as they also have the garden. Originally built in the eleventh century on the ruins of a Benedictine monastery, this was the Abbey of Notre Dame of the Grotto, and was built for the Bishop of Vence. How they did look after themselves! The present family, the Lavoillotte, have restored it into a museum of perfumes and aromas, because the previous owner was a perfumer from Grasse.

I was first taken there by a colleague from Radio Riviera. The dining room itself is on the ground floor of the château, built in stone with wonderful timbers, stone arches and lovely candles burning everywhere. Tapestries are hanging on the walls and in the middle there is an ancient candle dipping/making machine.

The food is very well prepared and presented and for an occasion or a celebration it is something special. I must say we had a wonderful meal.

Food: 8   *Ambiance: 8½*   *Service: 7½*

On the route back to Cagnes-sur-Mer is a Scandinavian restaurant:

LA BROUETTE, 830 route de Cagnes

Tel: 93 58 67 16. Closed: Tuesdays.
Fixed price menus: F148 and F195. M and Mme Bornemann.

Not somewhere I would have chosen myself, but a retired Danish car dealer brought me. Out of season the owners operate the place by themselves. In season they take on extra help. The place is just off the main road and faces St-Paul-de-Vence. The interior is very Provençal with a fire burning, and the tables and chairs are rough hewn country pieces. We were offered an apéritif as we were choosing what to order. Many of the dishes are Scandinavian and those that are smoked the owner does himself. We both had the fixed price menu and a bottle of Entre-deux-Mers. The latter comes from the area between Narbonne and Toulouse. The meal was good: with our coffees we were offered an aquavit, and it all came to a little over 400 francs.

Food: 7½   *Ambiance: 8*   *Service: 7*

SAINT-PAUL-DE-VENCE

This little town is first noted in the tenth century and most of the building was then done by François Premier who wished to make a fortress to protect his frontier with the Var. The town has many legends, in fact too many to recount, but when you visit it you will be told some of them by the locals. The most famous restaurant in the town is certainly the Colombe d'Or. Many artists paid for their meals here by giving one of their works, so the auberge has a marvellous collection by Bonnard, Chagall, Matisse, Picasso, Utrillo and others. You have often read about it no doubt in various newspapers and magazines, with Yves Montand playing *boules* among the trees in front.

LA COLOMBE D'OR,
place du Général de Gaulle

Tel: 93 32 80 02. Closed 3rd November to 20th December.
Fixed price menu: none. M. Roux.

Certainly I don't find the quality merits the high price. But the reputation is there. Go and enjoy a drink under the fig trees on the terrace and if you get carried away have some lunch as well.

As St Paul is very fashionable most of the restaurants are rather pricey. Two other places of note are:

LA BARONNIE, 86 rue Grand

Tel: 93 32 65 25. Open only for dinner.
Fixed price menus: F275 and F375. François Szanco (chef).

MAS D'ARTIGNY, route de la Colle

Tel: 93 32 84 54. Closed: never.
Fixed price menus: F285 and F380. M. Scordel.

This hotel is the sister to the château d'Artigny in the Loire Valley. All the suites of the hotel have their own private pool, the style and decoration don't quite come up to that very special quality of the Châteaux in the Loire.

We now move on to the centre of the Côte d'Azur and its famous capital Nice, but before dealing with Nice itself there are a couple of places north-west of the city that I would like to mention. We are going north from near the airport on the N 202 to Digne and the ski resorts of Isola 2000 and Auron. On this road we get to St-Martin-du-Var where we find:

Jean-Francois ISSAUTIER, route N 202

Tel: 93 08 10 65. Closed: Sunday dinner and Mondays.

The place is simply him. He only offers one menu in the evenings at 400 francs though you can have his lunch time menu at 240 francs if you want to try out his talent. He is a true master-chef; his love is certainly cooking and making his clients happy.

A little further north you will come to:

LE PLAN DU VAR

Hotel CASSINI, route N 202

Tel: 93 08 91 03. Closed: Fridays.
Fixed price menus: F98 and F165. Joseph Martin and family.

This was one of my lucky finds. I usually read the *Nice Matin,* our local French daily newspaper, and from time to time I pick up a hint of something different. One particular day I read that a young man had just won the award for 'Apprentice of the Year for

Cooking'. I looked up the name of the establishment he worked at and found it wasn't mentioned in any of the guides. Yet how can any young man win this prize without a master to learn from? I decided to explore and booked a table for six and took a group of friends. You should have seen their faces when they learnt where we were going for dinner!

Joseph Martin and his sons are chefs, and good chefs at that. They have this small hotel, but they basically feed the locals and the passing trade. They prepare their own *foie gras* where others buy it in. They have an inexpensive set menu at 60 francs for three courses; the 98 franc menu is four courses and the 165 franc menu is six courses. The wine is very well priced. The Pays du Var cost 23/33 francs, but the first time I went they advised me not to choose that as it was a little rough; they felt I would be more than pleased with the Coteaux Varois at 32/45 francs. We followed their advice and were very satisfied with the quality. Two people can really have a super meal here at under 300 francs all in.

Food: 8½   *Ambiance:7 ½*   *Service:8 ½*

From just north of St-Martin-du-Var turn east on the CD 20, to La Roquette and:

LEVENS

LES SANTONS, 3 rue de l'Escalada

Tel: 93 79 72 47. Closed: Wednesdays.
Fixed price menus: F95 to F215. M et Mme Pellerin.

When I told Daevid, my radio colleague, what village we were going to talk about on the programme that particular day, he hooted and explained that was where his cricket team played their matches. In fact I had taken some Canadian friends there for lunch. We met on the N 202 as they were coming from Vence and I from Monaco. We arrived at this traditional local restaurant and were shown to the table I had reserved in the garden. Levens is a village perched well above the River Var valley and I was really expecting a view.

Sadly no, the garden was surrounded by a thick hedge. Thank goodness this was our only disappointment.

The restaurant offers four fixed price menus 95, 125, 148 and 215 francs. All offer five courses except the last that has seven. The 148 franc menu offers no choices, one just has to go through the card, as they say on the race track. The wine list is more than reasonable with the house wine being a Côtes de Provence AOC at 35/48 francs a half-bottle and a bottle. Usually you would be lucky to get a *vin de table* at this price.

There were olives and nuts to nibble on while we perused the menu. My Canadian friends had brought along their daughter. She, her mother and I chose the 125 franc menu, while her father went for the 95 franc one. Each menu offered as a starter an assortment of *amuse-bouche*. These included *quiche, tapenade, pâté de volaille* and several other tasters. John then had a pâté to begin with while we enjoyed parma ham with kiwi fruit, mussels cooked in a hazelnut sauce, and *quenelles* of salmon. All the dishes were well presented and it took one of my guests to point out that the plates were of lovely ironstone. My friend had the *gigot d'agneau*, his wife and daughter chose *lapin au pigeon* and I a *médaillon de lotte*.

When we were ready to order our desserts it was Monsieur Pellerin who came to advise and take our orders. What a choice! Fresh strawberries, black and white chocolate mousse (my daughters would have loved to be there), *pavé au chocolat* and *crème de marrons* with cream. That last dish was my father's favourite. I can always remember him having this with fruit salad every Sunday at the Chelsea Room in the Carlton Tower in London.

We had drunk two bottles of wine, two bottles of water, one Orangina and three coffees. Great value at 625 francs; under 160 francs a head.

Food: 8   *Ambiance: 6½*   *Service: 7½*

The Pellerins came from Paris twenty-five years ago. They worked on the coast until ten years ago when they purchased this restaurant. They are gradually building a regular clientele, from as far away as Italy. I want to wish them every success.

Chapter Ten
NICE AND ENVIRONS

Nice is the oldest and largest town, now a city, on the Côte d'Azur, originally founded by the Greeks of Marseille around 350 BC. It nestles in an amphitheatre of hills. Its attraction was certainly its position and climate. The valley of the River Var, at its western edge, has four harvests per year. The Romans then colonised Cimiez further east with a port which is now the quai des Etats-Unis. Cimiez was erased during the invasions of the Barbarians and Saracens.

Nice began to develop again in the tenth century under the Counts of Provence. During the fourteenth century it again saw change when the two adopted sons of Queen Jeanne, Countess of Provence, arranged for her to be suffocated then fought between themselves for the title. The Count of Savoy saw this as the moment to install himself in Provence and Nice, which then remained part of Savoy until 1860 (except for a few short breaks). Nice was occupied by French troops in 1792 and Napoleon came and stayed several times in the rue St Francois de Paul, just in front of the opera. The House of Savoy regained it in 1814 with the fall of the Empire. Napoleon III received Nice and Savoy for helping Sardinia clear the Austrians from Northern Italy. A plebiscite was held in 1860 under the orders of Victor-Emmanuel II, King of Sardinia, 'without any constraint on the will of the people'. The Niçois voted to become part of France, with 25,743 for and only 260 against.

There were several great men of Nice, including Massena who became Marshal of France and was rated by Wellington as the best general of France after Napoleon. One of the principal authors of the Italian Revolution, Garibaldi, was born here. One could go on, as the history of Nice has been very colourful. Many monuments remind us of this history, including the Roman arena and baths; there are great churches, a lovely Russian example; marvellous museums including those of great artists who came to live here. But we are going to talk about the food, as over the centuries Nice has played an important role in the development of different dishes.

The food of Nice is a mixture of the influences of sea and mountains, developed over time by the passage of foreigners and the local housewives and, in the last century, perfected by great chefs. The dishes are of great variety since the locality has an abundant choice of raw materials to draw upon. There is a mixture of vegetables and salads from the coastal plains, olive oil, beef, pork, cream and herbs from the surrounding mountains and fish at its feet in the sea. Niçoise cooking, they say, is a *mélange* of French and Italian cooking with a flavour enriched by the herbs of Provence. These herbs not only add flavour but enhance it with a noble aroma. The rustic and refined are rolled into one. The sun and sea have helped create all the primary foods; everything is eaten: leaves and flowers, stems and roots.

Among the famous dishes that originated in this area the most well known is *salade Niçoise* which is found on menus all over the world. Most people have also heard of *ratatouille* and a few have heard of *estocaficada* and *pissaladier*. These and others are local dishes where recipes have been handed down from mother to daughter. I am going to explain some of these to you and point you to traditional restaurants that serve them.

Daube – a form of stew with braised beef, tomatoes, onions, carrots, mushrooms, red wine, country maize, and flavoured with herbs.

Estocaficada – stockfish that is not local but comes from northern countries. The ships that carried olive oil north could not return empty, so they came back loaded with this dried and salted fish, which was cheap and did not rot. The Niçois created their most original dish using tomatoes, onions, new potatoes, sweet peppers, local black olives, all combined together with the fish as a *ragoût*.

Courgettes au Gratin – using sliced courgettes, sliced potatoes, herbs and grated cheese placed in the oven and cooked slowly. Our children first fell in love with courgettes when our housekeeper gave them this dish except that her version had tomatoes and plenty of garlic. If you ate her dish once a week you never caught a cold all winter.

Polenta – to me an Italian dish made from semolina of maize boiled in salted water and seasoned with butter and parmesan cheese and served with the juice from a roast or eaten with sausages.

Porchetta – a milk fed suckling pig stuffed with its own gizzards and tripe, flavoured with sage and thyme.

Pissaladier – an onion tart similar to a pizza, with anchovies and olives.

Sanguin – orange-coloured mushrooms that grow in the shade of pine trees, sautéed in olive oil, garlic and covered with white wine and thyme.

Socca – a biscuit made from the flour of chick peas with water and olive oil, cooked at a high temperature in a charcoal oven and usually served with *pissaladier* or *tarte aux blettes*.

Tian – an omelette made from vegetables that are currently in season and flavoured with basil and parsley.

Mesclun – a salad made from the herb rocket, young leaves of oak, young lettuce leaves and a little chervil, and dressed to flavour.

Some of the above dishes sometimes do not sound so tempting yet when you try them out you are surprised how good they are.

I am going to list some of the restaurants that serve Niçois food:

DON CAMILLO, *5 rue des Ponchettes*

Tel: 93 85 67 95. Closed: Sundays and Mondays.
Fixed price menus: F270 to F360. Franck Cerutti.

Franck Cerutti produces the finest and most delicate food of this town. He may have a more Italian flavour, as this thirty-year-old young master spent some of his apprenticeship there. Not cheap but Number One.

BARALE, 39 rue Beaumont

Tel: 93 80 52 50. Closed: Sundays and Mondays.
Fixed price menu: none. Meal costs 200 francs. Hélène Barale.

Hélène Barale was born in this very building nearly eighty years ago and is still running this famous establishment. A meal will cost about 200 francs and it is closed on Sundays and Mondays.

CICION-MALLEN, 496 route de Pessicart

Tel: 93 84 49 29. Closed: Wednesdays.
Fixed price menus: F140 to F175. M. Mallen.

The fifth generation is now running this establishment. Their *hors d'oeuvres* are a speciality.

AU CHAPON FIN 1 rue du Moulin

Tel: 93 80 56 92. Closed: Sundays and Monday lunch.
Fixed price menu: F160. M. Loubes.

Monsieur Loubes comes from Carcassonne, but his Niçois cooking is excellent. He also has a menu from the south west.

LA MERANDA, 4 rue de Terrasse

Tel: NONE. Closed: Sundays and Saturdays.
Fixed price menu: none. Meal costs about 175 francs all in. Jean Giusti.

No telephone for this tiny place just up from the opera. You are elbow to elbow with many locals and increasing visitors. You cannot book so get there early and try pot luck.

LE SAFARI, 1 cours Saleya

Tel: 93 80 18 44. Closed: Sundays.
Fixed price menu: none. Meal costs about 200 francs.

Try to book a seat on the terrace in good weather.

L'ESCALINADA, 22 rue Pairolière

Tel: 93 62 11 71. Menus: from 100 francs.

LA CAMBUSE, Cours Saleya

Tel: 93 80 12 31. Fixed price menu: none.
Meal costs about 150 francs.

LOU BALICO, 20 avenue Jean-Baptiste

Tel: 93 85 93 71. Menus from 180 francs.

LOU NISSART, rue de l'Opéra

Tel: 93 85 34 49. Fixed price menu: none.
Meal costs just over 100 francs.

Now let me advise you on other good eating places in Nice. It is a large town so always be aware that cities are the same all over the world. You may be on holiday but thieves are not, so lock your car and don't leave anything in view. We always find it difficult after the reasonably good security of Monaco to be more aware when visiting other large towns along the coast.

Nice has a huge selection of restaurants. I am going to be more brief in my descriptions but I am going to give you a good variety. We have already discussed those that offer Niçois cooking; now those that offer fish as their main fare.

CAFE DE TURIN, 5 place Garibaldi

Tel: 93 62 29 52. Open: Every day dawn till 10 pm.
Fixed price menu: none. Meal costs 115–200 francs.

Don't bother telephoning as they don't reserve tables. Just turn up and if there are no tables you wait by the bar and have a drink. You could end up sitting with a prince on one side of you and a fellow who carries the vegetables in the market on the other. The last time we were there with a group of six we had opera singers on one side and ladies of the night on the other.

If you don't enjoy shell fish, mussels, etc. don't go. When they have allocated you a table you go and choose from the fresh selection exactly what you want to eat and this is then brought to you; from then on they serve you normally.

Everyone is very friendly and chatty.

The wine on offer is not a long list nor sophisticated. There is white Muscadet or Alsace, and as a red only Beaujolais. We had two whites and a red. We ordered two and half dozen large *Fines de Claire* oysters, a dozen clams, a dozen mussels, two large crabs, two dozen large and two dozen Mediterranean prawns plus a plate of cockles and winkles. All very fresh, delicious and luckily not very fattening. In all it cost about 200 francs each.

Food: 8½　　　　　*Ambiance: 8½*　　　　*Service: 8*

The next two places are very different from the last. These serve very good fish in lovely surroundings. They also offer several meat dishes, so you have a choice.

CHEZ MICHEL 'Le Grand Pavois', 11 rue Meyerbeer

Tel: 93 88 77 42. Closed: Mondays. Fixed price menu: None. Jacques Marquise and Joianna Ogner.

Jacques is the son of the originator of the restaurant Tetou in Golfe Juan and now his son runs it. Joianna is a Californian who moved to Nice as she fell in love with a Frenchman. Their fish, and certainly their *bouillabaisse*, is rated the best in Nice. I was on my own one particular Sunday and went there for lunch. I got talking to the gentleman next to me. It turned out that he owned the restaurant Côte de Boeuf and as it was his day to be closed he felt he wanted some fish and came here. He often came here for their lobster which is superb; that was his main dish on that Sunday.

The restaurant has many long-time regulars and the decoration is what I would call post-war France, reliable and solid. Many people want that because they know the place has kept its traditional values. The meal will vary in cost between two and three hundred francs, but it is good.

Food: 8½   *Ambiance: 7½*   *Service: 7½*

MAC MAHON, 50 boulevard Jean-Jaures

Tel: 93 62 30 71. Open: every day.
Fixed price menu: F170. M. Gamus.

Both the owner and the chef were at the leading hotel, the Negresco. Between them they have made a very popular fish restaurant. It is like an up-to-date brasserie. You can also have oysters, clams, etc. and their lamb with parsley is excellent. The price is in the same range as Chez Michel, between 200 to 300 francs for the meal.

Food: 8½   *Ambiance: 8*   *Service: 8*

LES DENTS DE LA MER,
2 rue St Francois de Paul

Tel: 93 80 99 16 . Open: every day.
Fixed price menus: F135 to F255. Charlie Bertoni.

Charlie is very welcoming and has a very well organised team of waiters to look after you. The place is like the inside of a galleon, which gives it a fantastic atmosphere. It fills up very quickly especially on weekends, so do book. Many go in large groups as it is noisy and fun. The 135 franc menu is three courses, there is a four course at 190 francs and six courses for 255 francs. Wines are surprisingly inexpensive for a place so well known and so central, just between the opera and the flower market. There is a great selection of fresh fish and *coquillages*.

Food: 8   *Ambiance: 8½*   *Service: 8*

The best restaurant in Nice is without doubt the main dining room of the Hotel Negresco. Here in a palatial room panelled in wood and decorated in Louis XIV style you are looked after in a manner that befits royalty:

CHANTECLER, 37 promenade des Anglais

Tel: 93 88 39 51. Closed: 19th November to 17th December.
Fixed price menus: F260 to F550. Dominique le Stanc.

Dominique, whom I have followed for close on ten years, is one of the great chefs. He is certainly a marvellous replacement for Maximin, who went off to open his own restaurant. He has a marvellous ability to create imaginative dishes, and his charming wife Danielle guides you gently through the choices. You always enjoy a memorable meal at the Chantecler. While you are there, remember to visit the English bar and the oval sitting room. Lovely mementoes of the past grandeur of 'THE' great hotels.

Food: 9½   *Ambiance 9½*   *Service: 9½*

LE BISTROT DU FLORIAN, 22 rue Alphonse Karr

Tel: 93 16 08 49. Closed: Saturday lunch and Sundays.
Fixed price menu: none. Claude Gillon.

Claude originates from Normandy which he abandoned six years ago to open the restaurant 'Le Florian' next door. The restaurant is one of tradition though he has just had it redecorated. The food is excellent and it has been rated a star this year in the *Guide Michelin*. Claude opened his Bistrot early in 1990 and he is like a small boy with a new toy. He organised that the main kitchen of 'Le Florian' should serve both the restaurant and the Bistrot. Every time I have been there he is busily looking after the customers in the bistrot. His daughter who looks after this part lifts her eyes in amusement.

It is great fun, decorated in brick, wood and antiqued mirrors. Wherever one sits one can follow the activity of the restaurant. The wine is reasonable, the food excellent, all for about F200 a head.

Food: 8   *Ambiance: 8*   *Service: 8*

LA TOQUE BLANCHE, 40 rue Buffa

Tel: 93 88 38 18. Closed: Sunday dinner and Mondays.
Fixed price menus: F135 to F260. Alain and Denise Sandelion.

Denise Sandelion gives you a very special warm welcome. She is wholesome and cuddly like my aunt Beattie. She and Alain come originally from Lyon, that centre of good restaurants, and worked in Grenoble for twenty years before heading south.

The restaurant has a very attractive décor, all the walls being in *faux-marbre*, clean and elegant. Most tables are round, which I find so much more comfortable to talk to all your party. Denise and an assistant serve you courteously and quietly; everything runs smoothly.

Both the 130 franc and 160 franc menus are three courses. We had the raw salmon as a starter and followed with *dos de dorade bonne femme*. The latter came with vegetables and a wonderful *pommes gratin dauphinois*; I do so enjoy potatoes in this manner. We passed over cheese in favour of dessert. My guest had *mousse au poire* and I a *compôte* of peaches and pears. Just right for a balanced meal. With a mineral water, wine and coffees the bill came to 460 francs.

Food: 8½   **Ambiance: 8**   **Service: 8**

L'A PROPOS, 3 rue de la Prefecture

Tel: 93 85 58 48. Closed: Sundays.
Fixed price menus: F105 and F155.

A lovely small restaurant right in the heart of old Nice. It is mainly used by Niçois at lunch times and it is then very full. Both menus on offer are three courses with a choice of cheese or dessert. The wines start at 35/55 francs for a Côtes de Provence, so even if you have the more expensive menu you come out spending less than 400 francs for two. A nice touch is they offer you After Eight chocolates with your coffees. I find now that more and more are doing this at the end of the meal.

Food: 7½   **Ambiance: 7**   **Service: 7**

The Hotel Beach Regency has been making some great efforts to improve its restaurants and still give good value. Most other hotels have improved their prices in relation to quality.

LE REGENCY, 223 promenade des Anglais

Tel: 93 83 91 51. Closed: July and August.
Fixed price menu: F235. Gérard Ferri (chef).

The hotel has several restaurants; Le Regency is closed in the summer but La Piscine restaurant on the roof by the pool is then open and offers a beautiful setting above Nice on a summer evening. The hotel serves about three thousand meals a week so the food has to be fresh and top quality. The menu includes four courses and has about five different dishes to choose from per course. A business luncheon at this price all-in is good value, and the variety of dishes is first class.

Food: 8½   *Ambiance: 8*   *Service: 8*

They also have special weeks when they offer meals from different parts of the world, and a luncheon club that is attractive to join if you eat business lunches very regularly. Telephone Patrick Libs, Directeur de Restauration.

FLO-NICE, 4 rue Sacha Guitry

Tel: 93 80 70 10. Open: every day.
Fixed price menu: F145. M. Mercier.

Group Flo have just purchased an excellent site in the centre of Nice. They are well known restaurateurs who have brasseries in Paris and several other European cities. The site they have acquired was a restaurant, but had originally been built as a theatre in 1897 and was where they staged the Folies Bergères in Nice.

The restaurant seats well over a hundred and has the kitchen behind glass on the original stage. They offer a wide range of dishes, and they specialise in shell-fish. The chef, Jean-Paul Peluffo, is the fifth generation in his family to be involved in the preparation of food.

Now for those places that are a little different or in a more distant *quartier*.

LE GRAND CAFE DES ARTS,
Musée d'Art Moderne

Tel: 93 80 58 58. Open: every day. Fixed price menu: none.
Jean and Helen Thomas.

You do not have to go to the Museum to eat here. The restaurant is also open at night when the museum is closed. It serves good French food with no trimmings and the French would call it *très efficace*. The prices are reasonable for both food and wines. You should have a good meal for two with wines and coffee for about 260 francs.

There is also a terrace facing the new Theatre. A wonderful situation. They are very modern; when they take your order they punch it into a portable machine, like a calculator. This places your order straight away in the kitchen and enters it on your bill at the cashier.

Food: 7½   *Ambiance: 8*   *Service: 7½*

LE RAJA, 2 boulevard Carnot

Tel: 93 89 57 36. Open: every day. Fixed price menu: F200.

The 200 franc menu includes Raja Thali (several different specialities), Sizleek as a main course (mixed grill), sorbet or fruit salad, apéritif, wine and coffee are all included in the price. This is North Indian cuisine with a little French accent. The food is of excellent quality in a delightful setting at the edge of the old port. Even if you eat *à la carte* you come out with a bill of about 200 francs.

Food: 8   *Ambiance: 8*   *Service: 8*

AUX GOURMETS, 12 rue Dante

Tel: 93 96 83 53. Closed: Sunday evenings and Mondays.
Fixed price menus: F146 to F240.

This is a restaurant of the *quartier* of west Nice very near to the University. Stick to the 146 franc menu and you won't be sorry. Two of us started with fish soup and *coquilles St Jacques* followed by a pepper steak and an *escalope de foie-gras*. We had dessert and coffee and a bottle of Côtes de Provence St Maur red. We gave the small change from the four hundred francs we had placed in notes, as a tip.

Food: 8   *Ambiance: 7½*   *Service: 7*

LA NISSARDA, 17 rue Gubernatis

Tel: 93 85 26 29. Closed: Sundays.
Fixed price menus: F56 to F120. M. Prunier-Grossin.

The 56 franc menu is only at lunch time, with that and a *pichet* of wine and coffee your bill will come out at 73 francs. In the evenings there are F68, F88 and F120 menus to choose from. More Italian than French, yet they do dishes like *tripe à la niçoise* and pheasant with *foie-gras*. Here you certainly won't starve and your pocket won't be picked clean.

LE FLORIDE, 52 boulevard de Cimiez

Tel: 93 53 11 02. Closed: Saturdays and Sundays.
Fixed price menu: F80. M. Terese.

This little restaurant is open for lunches only in the week. I can't understand how they make enough money to live. The 80 franc menu is great value and they are open only for five lunch times. You will enjoy a lunch under the trees on the smartest street in town.

Having visited Nice we are now going to look at some of the villages in the hills just north of the Côte d'Azur. The one furthest north is about 65 kilometres from Nice. Continue on the road we took to Plan du Var, the N 202, and then the D 2565 to:

SAINT-MARTIN-VESUBIE

This village, at the extremity of the mountain pass, housed a Benedictine monastery as early as the third century. It later fell to the Ligurians and the Romans before returning to the Benedictines who founded the Sanctuary of Our Lady of the Windows. The village still celebrates many religious festivals, and on some of these their most treasured twelfth century Madonna is paraded from the Sanctuary to the church.

Today the village is a summer mountain resort, but very lovely to visit, especially in the autumn. There are several places to enjoy a good lunch and then walk through the hills. The village is at an altitude of 1,000 metres so go prepared with warm clothes.

LE CHAMOIS

Altitude 1000. Tel: 93 03 31 98. Closed: Winter (telephone).
Fixed price menu: F120.

This is a true French restaurant without any fuss, with the menu on a blackboard for all to see. The choice is limited to four starters, five main dishes and several desserts. The wines are reasonable as well in that several start at 60 francs, including a Côtes du Rhône or a Côtes de Provence.

The place seats about thirty so if you intend to go walking in the Vallée des Merveilles and you want some lunch, please book.

My guest started with a *salade exotique* that contained crab with a curry sauce, I the salad of smoked breast of goose with haricot beans. Both fine flavours, and the aroma of the curry tempted me to have a taste – just as delicious as my dish. Another thing that is delicious and special is the bread, baked locally, called a Michette, coiled a little like a plait. Before our main course arrived the owner showed us *la folie du Chamois*, which he was taking to another table and which consisted of a fillet of beef and half a lobster both prepared in an armagnac sauce. He pointed out that it added 50 francs to the menu price. Our mixture of prawns, Saint Pierre (John Dory) and mussels all on a bed of *poivrons* with a light sauce never compared, though we both thought it excellent. Both of us finished with one of my favourites, *tarte Tatin* with fresh double cream. We had drunk a couple of beers, a bottle of Badoit and four coffees and the bill came to 336 francs.

Food: 7½   **Ambiance: 7**   **Service: 7½**

The drive back is also a delight; the colours created by the sun setting in the west give everything that warm Provençal glow.

NICE-EZE

On the Haute Corniche, the old road that travels at the top of the hills overlooking the sea between Nice and Eze is one of my favourite places, summer or winter, somewhere we keep going back to time and time again. and we have never been disappointed. I lie, I have telephoned to book and found it was already full.

LA CHAUMIERE,
384 boulevard de l'Observatoire

Tel: 93 01 77 68. Closed: Sundays.
Fixed price menu: F350. Madame Nicole Cere.

This welcoming country place seems expensive, yet it is never empty. Even in mid-winter it has its regulars. Customers are even more numerous when the season is in full swing or there is a festival or large conference. It is listed in address books belonging to people all over the world. There is no written menu; the first question you are asked is what colour wine you require? The second whether you want beef or lamb and what *cuisson* (how well done you want it).

The terrines and plates of food are placed on your table. They include pâté, mushrooms and onions in a sauce, finely sliced *jambon St Michel*, niçoise olives and a basket of the freshest and firmest vegetables, glistening as if they have had their skins wax-polished. With this come wonderful country slices of bread toasted and ever-so-slightly burnt on the open fire.

I have forgotten to tell you more about the place itself. This was because the first thing that comes to mind is the food. The place has old beams, wonderful copper pans and other kitchen implements hanging from the beams and walls. Tiled floors, upright wooden chairs with straw seats complete the country style. You go there casually dressed; for some people that means with gold chains and the latest from Dior, Chanel, Karl Largerfeld or some flamboyant Italian designer.

The meat arrives, the beef slightly burnt on the outside and wonderfully pink on the inside, the chef's sharp knife giving you slices that melt in your mouth. The lamb is well flavoured with rosemary. I have difficulty writing this as I am so tempted to stop, get in the car and drive up to the Haute Corniche.

The meat comes with a jacket potato which has been well cooked in the red-hot embers of the fire. There is more salad for those that desire it, this time with the house dressing. Monsieur the chef, who is not part of the family (or so he says), stands in front of a simple fireplace that emits an enormous heat. If you have a table near the fireplace the ladies on the side closer to it will love it in winter, but demand to be some distance from it in summer.

The cheese tray is offered to you. Take a small slice, just to give you a taste. Now to the desserts. There is always a good choice of tarts, fresh fruit such as strawberries or raspberries, or a quarter of pineapple and others. Then Madame places this churn of thick Normandy cream on the table and tells you to help yourself to as much as you want, but don't make yourself sick. Surprisingly, there are few places that offer this sort of cream especially in the south. You now need someone to carry you out as you have eaten so much good food. The whole thing costs about 400 francs a head all in. This isn't cheap but it certainly isn't expensive for what you get, since the quality of everything is first class.

I have taken friends from all over the world to this restaurant and they are duly impressed. A good Italian friend, Erminio, has lived in Monaco for many years, yet even though he is a large exporter of meat he had never been here. We went together to the Chaumière one evening and he talked about the quality of the beef and lamb for many months afterwards.

Food: 9 *Ambiance: 8½* *Service: 7½*

LA TRINITE-NICE

AUBERGE LES PIERRES LONGUES,
rue Laghet, quartier Lavelent

Tel: 93 54 40 60. Closed: Wednesdays.
Fixed price menus: F75 to F150. Jean-Marie and Chantal Biscroma.

Coming from La Turbie you follow the road to La Trinité; if you get to the large supermarket, Auchan, you have gone exactly three kilometres too far. Coming from Nice you get to Nice-Est then aim for La Trinité – Auchan, and you know the way from there.

There are three four course menus, at F75, F115, and F150. There is a five-course menu for 250 francs. The wines are middle-of-the-range prices and there is a good selection. This is a good place to go with a group of friends.

Food: 7 *Ambiance: 7* *Service: 7*

LA TURBIE

This small town is situated above Monaco on the original Roman Way, so this road was the frontier town joining the old state of Rome with its province Gaul. You certainly won't be the first to tread this route. The large monument was built in 6 BC by the Roman Senate to mark the success of Emperor Augustus over all the Gauls. It was named a TROPHEE and regarded as a symbol of peace. After the fall of the Empire it was continually damaged until eventually most of its stones were used in the building of the church of Saint Michel in the eighteenth century. The present Trophée is a reconstruction dating to early this century, financed by an American art dealer, Edward Tuck.

HOTEL NAPOLEON, 7 avenue Victoire

Tel: 93 41 00 54. Fixed price menus: F115 to F190.

This hotel on the high street of La Turbie always offers fine fare. Sadly the dining room is rather functional so I have never felt the place had *chaleur*, as the French would say. The menus are good and the wine list offers a good selection starting at 30/50F for the local half-carafe or carafe.

The least expensive menu had four starters: *salade Niçoise*, a vegetable pâté, *tagliatelle aux fruits de mer*, and grilled red peppers. Last winter I had a fabulous soup of *moules en croûte*, a bowl full of mussels in a thick broth and the whole bowl covered by pastry. This time we followed with a *suprème de volaille aux champignons* and an *emincée de boeuf sauce Roquefort*. I had cheese and my guest *crème caramel*. With a carafe of rosé and two coffees we came away with change from three hundred francs.

Food: 7½   *Ambiance: 6*   *Service: 7½*

The good news is that from late spring 1992, La Turbie will become a much quieter village as the new tunnel from the *autoroute* to the Moyenne Corniche is due to open. The village will certainly become more pleasant to live in and walk around.

PEILLE

From La Turbie go on the D 55 then the D 22. From Nice go up the N 201 and turn onto the D 53. You will be surprised to learn this little village was the seat of the Counts of Provence, so it has an interesting history plus some fascinating buildings. A worth while visit and a good excuse to eat at:

LE RELAIS CHEZ COTTON,
Quartier St Martin de Peille

Tel: 93 41 16 03. Closed: Wednesdays and Thursday dinner.
Fixed price menu: F150 (F60 for children). Cotton.

Cotton is a large man with an impressive black beard who imposes himself over this large country restaurant overlooking the harsh countryside around. The restaurant itself is like a large, well-organised farmhouse.

The 150 francs set menu is five courses. To be able to eat it all you must arrive hungry and the best bet is to get out for a good long walk after. There is a wide selection of dishes and these are generally wholesome. The staff are friendly and professional and on hand all the time. Wines are just below the middle bracket.

My daughter Victoria had been lumbered with me that particular day and as the sun was shining we decided to take a walk in the hills around Peille. I knew where we would end up so I took the precaution of booking for about one o'clock. At the appointed hour, by pure chance!! we arrived at the entrance to Cotton's Place.

We were ushered to our table, and immediately I looked at the wine listed and ordered a bottle of Cave Audemar Côtes de Provence rosé and a bottle of still mineral water. The lady who was taking the order indignantly told me if we wanted still water the local mountain stream was better for us and fresher. Sheepishly we had to agree. We perused the menu while we sipped the wine. The first course offered *jambon, sanguin* (type of mushroom), terrine, *salade*. Victoria had the *salade* and I the *sanguin*. Then a choice of *truite d'amande, lasagne* and for us the ravioli and *écrevisse*. The main course choice was *lapin, caille, faux-filet, foie de veau*, or my daughter's *veau allouette* and my *civet de chevreuil*. Cheese; we were visibly slowing down the rate of absorption. For dessert the selection included *tarte au citron* or *tarte Tatin, profiteroles* with plenty of ice cream and several other items to make your mouth water. Victoria, having resisted all that was rich throughout the meal, fell to the temptation of the *profiteroles* for dessert and I, being regularly boring, took the *tarte Tatin*, with ice cream of course. I finished my meal with a wonderful strong espresso coffee. I needed that injection of caffeine.

The bill came to 361 francs . . . **No credit cards are accepted here!** Bring money or a French cheque book.

Food: 8 *Ambiance: 8* *Service: 8*

Many places in the south have complicated opening and closing days, this is no exception. In fact I feel this is really complicated so I am listing it in detail:

Annual closure: 30th October till 24th November. *From 1st May to 17th September:* open for lunch and dinner except Wednesdays and Thursdays. *18th September till 30th April:* open only at lunch times except Wednesdays.

PEILLON

AUBERGE DE LA MADONE. In the village

Tel: 93 79 91 17. Closed: Wednesdays.
Fixed price menus: F120 to F280. M. Millo.

Of all the perched villages in the south of France, Peillon in the hills behind Nice must be the most perilously perched of all. But the winding drive to the top is well worth it for the views and a chance to eat on the pretty terrace of the Auberge de la Madone just above the medieval village square. The Millo family who run this hotel and restaurant provide delicious and fresh fare at a reasonable price. We enjoyed a large and varied salad (*salade de primeurs au fromage blanc*), almost Italian in style (we are only a few miles from the border), good *rascasse*, traditional rabbit and lamb. Desserts include a simple but delicious peach tart, *meringue vacherin* and sorbets.

The auberge also has 15 rooms for those who do not want to hazard the drive back down the mountain after dinner.

Food: 7½ *Ambiance: 7½* *Service:7*

Now we move back to the coast.

Leaving Nice by the Basse Corniche with the sea on your right, the well-built hillside on your left is Mont Boron. You will come to a sharp left hand bend and in front of you, across an expanse of water, you will notice a lighthouse, which is on the headland of Cap-Ferrat. The expanse of water is the immense bay of Villefranche. This is one of those rare creations of nature, a horseshoe bay surrounded by hills. In summer this amazing bay is full of yachts of all sizes and shapes. In fact it can hold several naval vessels, including an aircraft carrier, at the same time. The saying goes 'still waters run deep' and this is true of this place as the water is over sixty metres in depth.

VILLEFRANCHE-SUR-MER

When you leave the main road and head down towards the sea you will come to this picturesque town tucked in below the hillside and at the water's edge. It isn't as old as one might imagine, in fact it was Charles II of Anjou who gave it commercial freedom in the fourteenth century and from this it acquired its name. Charles was also the Count of Provence and nephew of Saint Louis, that great king of France.

Its next mention in history was in 1538 when Pope Paul III (previously mentioned when we talked about Vence) called the Congress of Nice, in order to bring peace between the Emperor Charles V and his brother-in-law Francois I. The former was anchored in the bay of Villefranche and the other staying at Villeneuve-Loubet. The story goes that the Queen of France visited her brother on his ship in the port. The Emperor with the Duke of Savoy and their retinues came out on to the gangplank to greet her. There was an almighty C-R-A-C-K and they all ended up in this wonderful bay. The peace, sadly, only lasted five years.

The impressive Citadel was built for the Duke of Savoy in 1560 and it now houses the Town Hall, a museum to the sculptor Volti, and a meeting place. This was never a well-placed fortress as the first attackers found it was easy to come from towards Nice over the hill and the fortress was simply penetrable below them. The second fort, that you see at the top of the hill, was then built.

Villefranche remains a picturesque small town with narrow streets. There are regular antique and bric-à-brac fairs. As it is so wonderfully situated by the water's edge many restaurants have sprung up. Our favourite is one on its own at the top of the bay:

CARPACCIO, plage des Marinières

Tel: 93 01 72 97. Closed: Tuesdays. Fixed price menu: none.

The situation is certainly what first attracts you to this restaurant. There is also parking right nearby, so you don't have to walk half way round the bay. The name comes from the Italian dish of raw fillet steak sliced very thin, like smoked salmon, with thin pieces of parmesan cheese, and garnished with a little olive oil and maybe a little lemon juice.

Seated on the terrace facing the bay with the open sea in the distance, one is well protected in winter from any breeze and facing the sun; in summer one needs shelter under a parasol. It is extremely popular at lunch times in winter and evenings in summer. There is an interior that is surprisingly very comfortable and welcoming. The owner Michel and all his staff are true professionals, so you are well looked after, and you will find the food excellent.

Sadly there is no set menu. The *à la carte* offers a good variety of both fish and meats, and the portions are ample. A plate of *carpaccio* is a must and a plate of true *pommes frites* in accompaniment makes it even more memorable. The wines are reasonable and a good selection, starting with a *pichet* of house wine at 35 francs for 50 cl. A full three course meal comes out at about 250 francs, and you won't be disappointed.

Food: 7½   **Ambiance: 8**   **Service: 7½**

Going back to the old port, you find just facing the bay the Welcome Hotel. If you stay here in season you are obliged to take demi-pension. Mind you, this is no hardship as the restaurant on the front terrace is first class and called the:

SAINT-PIERRE, quai Courbet

Tel: 93 55 27 27. Closed: end Ocober to Christmas.

If you mount to the other side of the hotel and go up one of the tiny streets, you will come to a cross street, the rue du Poilu. Here you will find:

LA GRIGNOTIERE, 3 rue du Poilu

Tel: 93 76 79 83. Closed: Sundays and lunchtimes.
Fixed price menus: F110 and F150. Michel and Isabel Rhodes.

Michel and Isabel run this tiny cosy restaurant themselves and offer two menus, one of three courses at 110 francs and a four course at 150 francs. You have practically the same except for the extra course, for which my guest chose *moules marinières*, after our start with a fish salad and a vegetable pâté. We then both chose the salmon trout as our main course even though there was a variety of other dishes offered. I chose several cheeses from the platter and my guest went for the *crêpe coulis de manderine du jardin* that looked wonderful.

We drank the Réserve du Maison, a house white that was every bit as good any of the Côtes de Provence on the list. It was priced at 75 francs which I class just above middle of the road. The Chablis at 150F I found to be on the high side for this type of establishment. Stick to the house choice.

We had enjoyed a menu at each price, the wine and two coffees and the bill came to 355 francs which I found to be great value.

Food: 8   *Ambiance: 8*   *Service: 8*

If you go back to the Corniche and head eastward in the direction of Monaco you will come to the avenue Leopold II. Go up this road until the first turning, that happens to be a hairpin bend to the left. The house at the apex is:

LE MASSOURY, avenue Leopold II

Tel: 93 01 03 66. Closed: Wednesdays.
Fixed price menus: F290 to F480. Jean-Max Haussy

This villa with a terrace that has a spectacular view of the Bay of Villefranche, offers superlative cuisine in the setting of the early decades of this century. The plates and glasses that adorn the tables are all different, which I must say I find unusual and interesting. Prices are in the same bracket as the Chantecler in Nice from where Monsieur Haussy came.

CAP-FERRAT

This piece of land, pointing into the Mediterranean between Villefranche and Beaulieu, houses some of the most expensive properties in the South of France. Several are palaces, built for their original owners who were kings and princes. The man who built several wonderful homes here was the King of the Belgians, Leopold II. At around the turn of the century he was reputed to be the wealthiest man alive. He personally owned the African State known as the Belgian Congo, which was brimming over with minerals, including precious stones and metals. The museum Ile de France, a villa that straddles the high point of the Cap with a view of both the Bay of Villefranche and the Bay of Beaulieu is worth a visit and houses the collection of Ephrussi de Rothschild.

On this famous promontory there are two superb hotels. The Hôtel du Cap is situated at the end and has a funicular to take you down to its restaurant and the beach, and La Voile d'Or overlooks the old fishing port. Both these places have restaurants to match their five star standing. There are several other establishments in or near to the main town of St-Jean-du-Cap-Ferrat; I would recommend you to try:

LE SLOOP, *Nouveau Port du Cap-Ferrat*

Tel: 93 01 48 63. Closed: Wednesdays and Sunday evenings out of season. Fixed price menu: F165. Alain Therlicocq.

Alain is a chef of note, having won the Prix Pierre Tattinger, among other prizes, for his cooking. He opened this restaurant in the new port of St Jean several years ago and it is certainly a surprise to find a place of this calibre so close to moored boats. He offers a menu of five courses for 155 francs, which is excellent value for money, but his wines start at over 100 francs which is on the top side regarding prices.

The fixed price menu has several choices in each course but to give you an example of an excellent meal, the last time I ate there I had *biscuit de loup fourré de langouste fraîche*, (sea-bass stuffed with langouste) followed by a light *feuillette d'asperges* (asparagus in a puff pastry), then on to a *risotto de selle d'agneau rôti sauce purée foie gras*. Just the words describing each plate are a piece of prose. Cheese and then dessert and coffee. If two of you have the fixed price menu, that comes to 330 francs but a bottle of wine, just a simple Cassis rosé is 125 francs and your two coffees bring it to a total of 475 francs. Yet this is good when you consider the quality and the service. If you don't have the fixed price menu one meal will certainly be more in the region of 300 francs.

Food: 8½   *Ambiance: 7½*   *Service: 8*

It is certainly a more pleasant place when the weather is good and one is seated on the terrace surveying the boats and the activity surrounding them.

BEAULIEU-SUR-MER

This is just due east of Cap-Ferrat. It has a lovely casino which is closed at present, and the Villa Kerylos is a must if you wish to see a reconstructed Greek villa. There are several hotels, the most well known being La Réserve, which has a regular clientèle. The place to eat is traditionally the port where one finds several restaurants offering pizzas, pastas and more sophisticated dishes, the most well known being the African Queen. None is good value but on warm days in winter or lovely evenings in summer, most are full.

EZE

This town is split into two, Eze-sur-Mer which is on the water's edge, (it is separated from the sea by the railway line), and Eze-Village perched on the top of a peak several hundred feet above. The latter must certainly be the most visited of all the perched villages of the South of France. Certainly you must swell the numbers and see the views to Italy, Corsica and St Tropez.

Eze was most probably built by the Phoenicians well before the Roman occupation. It was destroyed at the beginning of the eighteenth century by Louis XIVth during the wars of the Spanish Succession. The tree in the place de la Franche was planted by those who occupied the village during the French Revolution.

It has two well-known and expensive small hotel/restaurants in the old town and others in the vicinity:

CHATEAU DE LA CHEVRE D'OR, rue du Barrie

Tel: 93 41 12 12. Closed: Wednesdays and winter.
Fixed price menu: none. Meals cost about 500francs. Claude Hirt.

The view is spectacular and now they have a small annexe to the restaurant where you can lunch at a much cheaper price.

CHATEAU EZA, end of village

Tel: 93 41 12 24. Closed: Winter.
Fixed price menus: F250 and F480. André Rochat.

Monsieur Rochat bought this old château from the Prince of Sweden and restored it into an amazing small hotel perched at the very end of this precipitous village. You sit at your table on the balcony with the sea four hundred metres below. On clear days and nights the vistas are unsurpassable.

EZE COUNTRY CLUB, *route de la Turbie*

Tel: 93 41 24 64. Open all year.
Fixed price menus: F240 and F320. M. Lauthelier.

This is a new hotel built in the last five years to a very high standard. The restaurant is quite superb and in summer you can eat by the pool. There are also modern sporting facilities. You find it by taking the road towards Monaco out of Eze, and at the first left you take the direction of La Turbie. It is a few hundred metres on your right.

High above Eze on the Grande Corniche is another restaurant like a country farm:

LA BERGERIE, *Grande Corniche*

Tel: 93 41 03 67. Closed: Mondays. Fixed price menu: F170.

The moment you enter the door to this country establishment you encounter its comfort and warmth. It has a fire at the far end where the meat is hung to cook. Everything is relaxed. During one of those cold winters, around 1985, a group of us agreed to meet here for lunch the following Sunday. As we were going to be a large group of adults and children we booked a couple of days in advance. That Sunday dawned with heavy snow falling, but luckily several of us had four wheel drive vehicles. It was difficult to get to the restaurant due to the conditions, yet when we arrived we found everyone else had cancelled and we had the whole place to ourselves. Large fire, good company and delicious meat, what else does one need?

Back to the village of Eze where you can enjoy a simple meal at:

BELEZE, place Colette

Tel: 93 41 19 09. Closed: Sundays.
Fixed price menus: F65 to F140.

This village cafe/restaurant offers several menus between 65 and 140 francs. Wine is also reasonable, so if you are looking for an inexpensive lunch in the sun, you could do much worse. It is next to the car park on the Moyenne Corniche, with the old village imposingly above you.

EZE-SUR-MER

DU CAP ROUX, 34 avenue Liberté

Tel: 93 01 50 17. Closed: Wednesdays.
Fixed price menus: F90 and F130. Marie-P and Jean-C Schambacher.

The chef is Philippe Caine from Lyon, who was apprentice to the great Paul Bocuse, and you are served by his wife. The cuisine is a mixture of Lyonnaise and Provençal and even though the restaurant is on the main Basse Corniche going through Eze there are many regulars. Jean-Claud, the owner, took our order and helped serve throughout the evening. The place is decorated with blacksmith's tools and other such trophies from the earlier part of this century.

The wines are more than reasonable, considering you are on the sea-front, with the *cuvée du patron* at 19 francs a half-bottle/36 francs a bottle, and a good Côtes de Provence for 31/60 francs.

The 90 franc menu is quite impressive, with four plates to choose from in each course. The night we went you could start with *soupe de poisson, salade niçoise, mousse de foie de canard* or *coquilles St Jacques feuillettées*. For your main course there were *faux-filet, filet de rascasse, filet de loup poivre noir,* and *côtelette d'agneau aux herbes*. All these came garnished with hearts of artichokes, grilled tomatoes, potatoes, mushrooms and courgettes. Dessert or cheese. Not bad at all for 90 francs.

Food: 8   *Ambiance: 7*   *Service: 7*

The next point of call is naturally Monaco but before doing that I feel I should mention both Cap d'Ail (Garlic Head) and Beausoleil (Beautiful Sun). These two towns have grown in prominence due to being in such close proximity to Monaco. They are really dormitory towns to the Principality yet they have the total infrastructure of a normal town. Sadly they have very few restaurants, and of those they have, only a couple worth mentioning.

CAP D'AIL

Coming into Cap d'Ail along the Basse Corniche one is disappointed by the shops and buildings. The attractive villas are below or above this road and if you take the trouble to turn you will see some lovely homes. If you turn towards the sea you will come across:

PINEDE, 10 boulevard de la Mer

Tel: 93 78 37 10. Closed: Wednesdays and winter.
Fixed lprice menu: none. M. Louet.

This is certainly one of the best situations on the Côte as the restaurant is literally '*pied dans l'eau*', with the water breaking on the rocks in front. It serves mainly fish but sadly the food is not good value; in fact I find it pricey. They have a reasonably priced local wine but a Chablis costs over two hundred francs.

Another place clearly marked is a Pizzeria situated on the south side of the Basse Corniche on a corner. Here they serve general Italian dishes as well as the usual pizzas and pastas:

CHEZ MICHEL, 100 avenue de 3 Septembre

Tel: 93 78 34 01. Closed: Wednesdays.

BEAUSOLEIL

Very unlike Cap d'Ail this town has everything, including a good market that many people in Monaco use, as it is slightly cheaper. There are also a couple of good restaurants, but they aren't much cheaper than those in Monaco:

LE RESTAURANT, *9 bvd de la République*

Tel: 93 78 89 45. Closed: Saturday lunch and Sundays.
Fixed price menu: none. M. Verrene.

Monsieur Verrene is Swiss yet not new to restaurants in this area. He originally started the Pizza Monegasque, then owned Gianni's on the avenue Princesse Grace until rents got too high. He then bought this property and converted it into a good restaurant. It is very well decorated with several small dining rooms, the most interesting being the terrace that has a closing roof, and *trompe l'oeil* on the walls.

There is no set menu. Ten starters are priced at between F35 and 85 francs, main courses from F85 to 140 francs and desserts at F30 to 40 francs. If you have three courses it will cost between 150 and 265 francs. The surprising thing is the wine list. You can have a 50cl carafe at 33 francs or 75cl at 40 francs; the latter is equivalent to a normal bottle. Not bad at all. While we were ordering, they had placed slices of sausages and olives to nibble on; I always find this to be a nice touch.

The quality of the food is high and imaginatively prepared. I had a *friteur*, which is generally whitebait, but here it was a real mixture of several small fish including a couple of shell fish deep fried. My wife had started with a salad and followed with *scampi à l'huile d'olives* and I a *dorade au gros sel* that I shared with someone else. Four of us had eaten well and the bill, with the *dorade* the major portion of it, came to eleven hundred francs.

Food: 8½   **Ambiance: 8**   **Service: 7½**

Chapter Eleven
MONACO TO THE
ITALIAN BORDER

The Principality of Monaco is referred to as the gem of the Côte d'Azur. Many people also call it Monte Carlo, which is an error. Monaco is the true name of the Principality itself, which is split into four small towns: Monaco ville, which is the old town built on the rock, where one finds the Palace; the Condamine which is the part from the railway station and market square down to the old port; Monte Carlo, the part from the Hôtel de Paris and Casino eastwards to the end of the state; and lastly Fontvieille which lies to the west of the palace.

Squashed between the southern Alps and the sea, it occupies about 480 acres of which one-fifth have been reclaimed, mainly Fontvieille, from the sea. Fontvieille originated as a tiny beach, and here the first reclamation was done over a century ago to accommodate the power station, brewery and other industrial units. In the last twenty years a huge reclamation and development project has now made this area of Monaco into a large residential, recreation and business community.

The Principality may be tiny but it certainly offers everything. It is well known for its casinos and luxurious living, but not so well known for its concerts and ballet. The season starts in January with the Monte-Carlo Rally. February is the circus, a great favourite of HSH Prince Rainier. The tennis and golf competitions follow. At Whitsun there is the famous Grand Prix. Then there is the summer season, and the Fireworks competition, Red Cross Ball, Vintage

Car Rally, the Sailing Regattas, and many other occasions that really end with the Prince's birthday on the 19th of November.

Many people are regular visitors to Monaco, others just come for one day in their lives. The latter want to see the Palace, the Casino, and maybe someone famous, somebody they usually only read about in the Sunday tabloids. They want to make dreams come true.

I could go on but I should be directing you to places of culinary excellence. This state has 30,000 inhabitants, but it boasts over 150 restaurants.

My first choice is highly significant since without it this guide probably would not have been written. The restaurant in question is Castelroc, situated at the western end of the courtyard facing the Prince's Palace. The owner, a friend and shooting companion, had taken advertising time on the local English speaking station, Riviera Radio. The station wanted to interview him, but as he wasn't confident about his English he asked me to do the interview in his place. From this was born a regular restaurant review programme.

CASTELROC, place du Palais

Tel: 93 30 36 68. Closed: Saturdays and dinners.
Fixed price menus: F98 and F190. Francis Bonafed.

On the opening page of the menu is a good description of Monaco, written by Laurent Savelli, a man of letters. With Francis' permission I include a translation.

The Rock of Monaco

Take millions of tons of granite, coat them with about ten centuries, soak the whole lot into the Mediterranean, on the South-East coast of France a few leagues from Dante's fatherland. Then flavour with wild olive trees, agaves, dwarf palms, prickly pears, aloes, carob, cypresses, pine trees with their tasty kernels, and a few species of shrubs and 'succulent' plants.

Warm up in the southern sun and serve at lukewarm temperature.

Such is the recipe God invented when he created the Rock of Monaco, this ancient 'Roca' dear to Monegasque hearts and so admired by visitors from all over the world. Enter this friendly and welcoming 'CASTELROC' where, since 1913 you will be able to sample typical dishes of this famous historical site, and marvel at what I call 'angel cooking'.

For you are here in the very heart of the Principality, where the old fortress stood as sentry of the sea. In seven hundred years, the Grimaldi dynasty have made it into a marvellous and peaceful place. Here centuries are not crammed together, but blended intelligently and piously, from the clock tower to the apartments of each bygone era, through the ramparts and loopholes.

From the reign of the founder of the dynasty to the present of Rainier III, some of those who were the hosts of the Lords and later of the princes, have come back to life in their monuments. For example Charles V, the Duke of York, Benedict XIII the anti-Pope of Avignon, the Countess of Grignan, Machiavelli the famous Italian statesman and historian, the Empress of Hungary, wife of Emperor Ferdinand and a good friend of the princes of Monaco, Charlotte de Gramont, Queen Victoria-Eugenie of Spain and composers like Massenet and Saint-Saens.

Through Saint Martin's gardens, where the Knight of Lamark found his vocation as a botanist, you can view the magnificent Romanesque Cathedral, built in free stone from La Turbie and marble nearly a century ago on the site of the ancient church of Saint Nicolas. In similar style the Court House and the unique 'temple of the sea', the Oceanographic Museum, built by the Scientist Prince Albert I, and bequeathed on his death to that other great institute of science the Oceanographic Institute of Paris.

Just below the Porte-Neuve, Fort Antoine, built by an engineer of the Vauban School in memory of Prince Antoine

First. Back to the centre of the old city, where hidden by foliage is the Chapel of Peace. Today, by the wishes of Prince Rainier III, here is the tomb of his father the Artist, Prince Pierre of Monaco.

Going on with your tour you will come across the elegant building that houses the Ministry of State, then the Lycée Albert I from 1910, which originally was the Monastery for the Nuns of the Visitation in 1675, then the Jesuit College in 1802 and then the College of the Visitation in 1872. You have the Monaco Town Hall, originally the College of Saint Charles, one of its old boys being the poet, Guillaume Apollinaire, here from 1888 to 1896. The ladies' boarding school of Saint Maur's. The three hundred-year-old Chapel of Mercy, the Chamber of Deputies. And in the rue Comte Felix Gastaldi, over a doorway, a marble plaque stating it was the birthplace of Joseph-François Bosio, official sculptor to four French Monarchs, from Napoleon I to Louis Philippe. You can also wander through the picturesque alleys, arches and narrow streets, where the Middle Ages live at peace with the close of the twentieth century.

All around are the witnesses of the past, the ramparts, watch-towers, sentry boxes, canons and howitzers, some of which were royal gifts. All these relics of the past, respectfully kept by our Sovereigns and well protected by the Monegasques, recall irresistibly a poet's verses

   Lifeless objects, have you got a soul

   Which clings to our soul and the strength to love?

Following this quick tour, will you be able to tell whether the recipe you read at the beginning has allowed you to enjoy this tasteful dish?'

Now to sample the true recipes from their menu. There are two fixed price menus, one of three courses at 98 francs, which is very good value; and a five course menu at 190 francs which includes as starters smoked salmon and *foie gras*, and a choice of fish, meat, cheese and dessert to follow. The *à la carte* is varied and the choice of the fresh fish of the day is always excellent.

I am sorry to say I cannot help being biased. My other problem is whenever I go there I am never able to stick to the menus as Francis is always offering me this or that course to try out. Inevitably I try too many dishes, but I always enjoy myself. He is a good restaurateur from a family traditionally involved in this business. He is also both a gourmet and gourmand like myself. Often, if you are in the main market of Monaco, you will see him choosing the fruit and vegetables for that day. If he finds something different or special he will be offering it to his customers at lunch.

You will note from the above he is only open at lunch and is also closed on Saturdays. Because of its situation the restaurant is open for many hours at lunch times, with a very informal brasserie section where you can have a snack with a drink or a plate from the menu. In the restaurant area everything is much more traditional. The waiters have been with him for quite some time so you will be extremely well served. He is closed on Saturdays as it is his shooting day in the season – I forgot to tell you he is the local armourer. So he satisfies his two loves, food and shooting, lucky man. The restaurant also opens in the evenings when there is a concert in the Palace courtyard.

Don't forget they also offer local Monegasque specialities; in fact they usually put one of these before you as a taster while you are perusing the menu. Occasionally you may be lucky and see one of the Princes strolling across from the Palace to come and lunch or dine on the same terrace as yourselves.

The wine list starts at above my middle price range, about 75 francs a bottle for both Côtes de Provence and Côtes du Rhône. The wine list is long and good as this is another of Francis' hobbies. So if two of you go to lunch and have the three course menu, plus a bottle of Château St Martin, a bottle of mineral water and two coffees, your meal will cost 311 francs which is good value.

Food: 8   *Ambiance: 8*   *Service: 8*

Our family's special restaurant in old Monaco Ville is one we often go to in the evenings. We regularly take visitors who want an amusing meal with a group. This is to be found in one of the warren of tiny streets:

PINOCCHIO, 30 rue Comte Felix Gastaldi

Tel: 93 30 96 20. Closed: Wednesdays.
Fixed price menu: none. M. Fraceschini.

For those who don't know, the story of Pinocchio was written by the gardener at a well-known house, Collodi, near Florence in Italy. The story gained a wide following internationally with the cartoon film of that name by Walt Disney.

This is certainly a very different place, small and cosy inside during winter and outside on the narrow pavement facing a fountain in summer. It offers a variety of pastas with different sauces and a few other dishes. Wine is very reasonable at 30/50 francs upwards. You can have a very amusing evening for under 200 francs a head.

We normally have St Daniel ham, Mortadella, salami, etc. as starters, then a variety of pasta dishes from which everyone helps themselves. There are other main dishes and desserts. But if you want a lively evening, go there.

Food: 7   *Ambiance: 8½*   *Service: 7½*

Descending from the rock to the Condamine, and near the market square, the place des Armes, you will find a small street going towards the station and a speciality restaurant called:

LE PERIGORDIN, 4 rue de la Turbie

Tel: 93 30 06 02. Closed: Sundays.
Fixed price menu: F120. Gerard Baigue.

As the restaurant is small, Monsieur Baigue copes with all the service. He offers a three course fixed price menu and *à la carte*, recipes from Perigord, the area of France renowned for goose and duck, pâtés and of course foie gras. Your choice for the three course menu is from four starters, five main dishes and several desserts.

The main courses include *magret de canard, cassoulet, entrecôte, truite* or sole.

Wines are about middle of the price range, with the accent being on Bergerac, Cahors and others from East of Bordeaux. One needs the wine to have a stronger body and a more lasting nose to offset the richness of the food. Very different from local food which is light and full of sun.

Food: 8   *Ambiance: 8½*   *Service: 7½*

Down towards the water for something light and inexpensive, for those who are searching for a menu that does not tear a hole in your pocket. This is facing the port and the famous swimming pool, in fact on the starting grid of the Monaco Grand Prix:

DOLCE VITA, 25 boulevard Albert Ier

Tel: 93 30 99 10. Closed: Mondays.
Fixed price menu: F70. Joel Roy.

This is one of the places where the working population of Monaco lunch. They regularly have two *plats du jour* to choose from and the carafe of vin de Var only costs 25 francs. Joel will look after you well, exactly as he does his regulars.

You can stay on the Grand Prix track and go to the famous Rascasse corner, here you will find a restaurant of the same name. You can even book to spend the whole of Grand Prix day here:

LA RASCASSE, Port of Monaco

Tel: 93 25 83 00. Closed: rarely.
Fixed price menu: none, but plat du jour. *Rupert Stevenson.*

This restaurant, though well placed, remained closed for several years when I first arrived to live in Monaco. Rupert, who used to take it for corporate entertaining during the Grand Prix week, has now taken it permanently and made it a success. It is open as a bar and offers a *plat du jour* for lunch so that it now has many regulars.

The situation is second to none, great also for evenings when there is a firework display.

The restaurant offers mainly French food but there are a few Italian dishes. The wine list is middle of the road in price; its saving grace is a *pichet*, equivalent in quantity to a half-bottle for 30 francs. A good meal with a good wine sets you back between 225 and 250 francs.

Food: 7½   *Ambiance: 7½*   *Service: 7½*

The next restaurant is situated on the top floor of a car park! In fact this is a car park which has a mock Belle Epoque façade that looks over the port and the Palace. It is situated at the entrance to Monte Carlo.

SAINT BENOIT, parking de la Costa

Tel: 93 25 02 34. Closed: Mondays.
No fixed price menu. M. and Mme Athimond.

A beautiful restaurant, with a fabulous terrace, well situated considering the space problem in Monaco – it is on the top floor of this car park. So park your car and take the lift to the fifth floor.

It specialises in fish but has several meat dishes on offer. It is extremely well patronised by Monagesques and other locals. Prices are not cheap yet for the class of the establishment and for Monaco they are not expensive either. I do find the wine list on the high priced side, so choose wisely.

Food: 8   *Ambiance: 8*   *Service: 7½*

For something very different there is a Japanese restaurant of very high quality in the Hotel Metropole Gallery. On my first visit I was lucky enough to have a Japanese lady sitting next to me. We were both guests of a New Zealand friend who enjoyed Japanese cuisine. I had not been keen even though I had visited Japan a few years previously. I was a little wary of ordering a large variety of raw fish.

FUJI, 4 avenue de la Madone

Tel: 93 30 40 11. Closed: Sundays and Monday mid-day.
Fixed price menu: none. Kodela.

To start with I am going to give you a plain man's explanation of some of the dishes on offer. Please forgive me if I make some mistakes. First there is SASHIMI, these are usually appetisers or starters. They are all raw fish beautifully prepared and some are shaped in a decorative fashion. They have a delicate flavour and are served with a dip and a mustard paste. SUSHI on the other hand are always served with rolls of rice, all raw except octopus and shell fish. All the fish is perfectly filleted. TEPPANYAKI are grills and you sit at a table where there is a large flat grill plate as part of the table. The chef is flamboyant and very expert at cutting and preparing the dishes in front of you. an art form both in the preparation and the action.

My advice is to go and try an assortment of Sashimi or Sushi as a starter. The tunny fish looks strong as it is a deep colour, yet its taste and flavour has nothing to do with its colour. Drink a small carafe of the warm Sake. I am sure you will be impressed, you will enjoy it and you will go back. Or you could always just have the Tappanyaki.

Food: 9   *Ambiance: 8*   *Service: 7½*

A few Japanese translations to help you on your first visit:

Yes	*Haic*
No	*Ie*
More	*Moto*
Thank You	*Domo Arigato*
Please	You will have to find this one out for yourselves.

You can't visit Monte Carlo without at least having a coffee at the Café de Paris on the Casino Square. You can eat here from morning to night, and I love going there for the occasional meal. It is the place people go to look, to see and to be seen. You can watch the comings and goings for hours. And everybody goes there or goes past. Buy a paper, gamble or just simply look. It was completely gutted and rebuilt three years ago as a superb brasserie in the style of the Belle Epoque. You can garage your car nearby in the newly constructed car park under the gardens.

CAFE DE PARIS, Casino Square

Tel: 92 16 36 36. Closed: never.

Right opposite is the most famous Hotel in the Principality, and the best; The Hôtel de Paris. The Director, Dario dell'Antonia, was chosen as the Hotelier of the year in 1991. The hotel is the star of the S.B.M. (Société des Bains de Mer) group. As you mount the steps to enter, you can imagine who has done that before you, names from history books and the greatest from the world of the arts, theatre and film. As you enter you will encounter a large bronze of King Louis on horseback. People touch it for good luck. Sheer opulence surrounds you.

Yet a few years ago the S.B.M. group had really no restaurant of note. They have now changed all that, first by creating something that is almost without equal, and second by raising the standard of all the restaurants in all their hotels.

LE LOUIS XV, Hotel de Paris

Tel: 93 30 23 11. Closed: Tuesdays and Wednesdays.
Fixed price menus: F550 and F650. Chef Alain Ducasse.

The decoration is exquisite, the table settings fit for the finest homes and the food of unapproachable quality with an Italian/Provençal influence. The last is produced by a great young chef that we are going to hear a lot about in the future. This is the first and so far the only restaurant that the *Guide Michelin* has elevated to three stars where the chef is not the proprietor. No other words are necessary. If you don't want to eat there at least try to take a glance at this splendid room.

I have had the pleasure of sampling the delights from Alain Ducasse's kitchen and cannot give it too high praise.

LE GRILL, Hotel de Paris

Tel: 93 50 80 80. Open every day.
Cost: F600 to F900. Alain Ducasse.

Here on the top floor of the hotel is the traditional and famous Grill Room with its roof that opens and an uninterrupted view over the sea. There is as well the private room named after one of its famous visitors, Winston Churchill. The meats are indeed cooked over an open wood-burning fire, so the name is not just for effect.

The other dining room in the hotel is the Salle Empire. When the hotel opened the terrace to the Louis XV restaurant they found that extending the terrace for the Salle Empire room meant that its patrons would be below street level. This was not acceptable. They could not raise the terrace, so they in fact lowered the whole town square by about one metre, garden and all.

There are two other hotels in the Principality that belong to the S.B.M. Group: the Hermitage and the Mirabeau. The former is a very beautiful hotel and very comfortable, with a marvellous terrace. Certainly this terrace is a much better place for viewing the Grand Prix and the firework displays than elsewhere. The Mirabeau is more functional but has its own pool and is very well placed on the Grand Prix circuit; its restaurant has a very high rating in most gastronomic guides.

SALLE BELLE EPOQUE, Hotel Hermitage

Tel: 93 50 67 31. Open: all year.
Fixed-price menus: F290 and F380. M. Rauline.

LA COUPOLE, Hotel Mirabeau

Tel: 93 25 45 45. Closed: lunch in summer.
Fixed price menus: F250 and F360. Chef Joel Garault.

There are several other good restaurants in Monte Carlo that we regularly go back to, friendly places where, as a regular, they always welcome you with open arms.

SANS SOUCI, 42 boulevard d'Italie

Tel: 93 50 14 24. Closed: Sundays. Fixed price menu: none. Gianni.

The restaurant on avenue Princesse Grace still has the name Gianni; so when Gianni himself sold out and opened this new restaurant he had to choose another name. My wife says he produces the best *risotto aux cèpes* in the world, and I just adore his *hors d'oeuvres*, especially the anchovies in lemon. He offers the best wild mushrooms and asparagus in season, and his regular dishes of pasta with clams or the fresh fish are always good. We also sometimes just pop in for one dish at lunch times.

Food: 8   **Ambiance: 7½**   **Service: 7½**

POLPETTA , 2 rue Paradis

Tel: 93 50 67 84. Closed: Tuesdays.
Fixed price menu: F120. Brothers Guasco.

Another regular with the Roch Family and many of our friends. Good food and a lively atmosphere are the main recipes for an excellent meal. If only two of you go there to eat you will quickly be enlivened by the ambiance around you. The two brothers offer a wide selection of dishes that have a Franco-Italian flavour, they are also very welcoming. Occasionally a guitar player comes in to enliven the place further, and you can finish singing until the early hours. Great fun.

The places with the in-crowd are RAMPOLDI on avenue des Speluges just down from Casino square, and fifty yards further on GIACOMO. Both these are pricey yet very well patronised.

For something in a completely different field there is:

PULCINELLA, 17 rue du Portier

Tel: 93 30 73 61. Closed: Wednesdays.
Fixed price menu: none. Carlo Rossi.

This is certainly one of the best value for money restaurants in the whole of Monaco, and it has had that reputation for some years now. The owner Carlo is involved with other places but this is certainly the big success. It is always full so don't think you can turn up and have a table, especially when there is some event in the town. The food is good, the service functional and friendly, and the ambiance created by so many people being regulars and knowing each other. I can't remember going there and finding no one we knew.

This restaurant serves traditional Italian dishes. Starters include a whole variety of pastas, mozzarella and tomatoes, avocados with prawns, and other cold antipasti. Main course offers veal in breadcrumbs, steak, *osso buco*, thin grilled liver. For dessert there is fruit salad, tiramisu and *crème caramel*.

There is only one reason why I would recommend you not to go and that would be if you had a secret liaison.

Food: 7   *Ambiance: 7½*   *Service: 7*

My last recommendation in Monte-Carlo, is to another hotel. The Beach Plaza is certainly the best situated if you enjoy the beach and swimming. It is nearly at the end of the avenue Princesse Grace on the edge of the Principality. I personally enjoy being near the water when I go to a sea resort. It has its own private beach and pool and a couple of good restaurants.

LE GRATIN, Beach Plaza Hotel

Tel: 93 30 98 80. Closed: lunch in summer.
Fixed price menu: F250. Patrick Libs (Catering director).

If you have a business lunch, and you want to have a private conversation, this is certainly a place I would recommend. The meal is exceptionally good value as your menu includes everything. It is part buffet, part served meal.

The meal starts with an appetiser; the last time I went we were offered a *beignet de fleur de courgette*. You then help yourselves to the first course, which includes smoked salmon, Parma ham, and a wide selection of *hors d'oeuvres*. The main course is either roast beef, another roast or a *plat du jour*. The other roast was lamb, and the '*plat*' was tagliatelle with smoked salmon. Cheese and a choice of desserts follow. Coffee and wine were also included. I think 250 francs per person very good value, especially when you add all the trimmings you get from a first class hotel.

FONTVIEILLE

Our last ports of call are here actually in the port of Fontvieille. As mentioned earlier this whole area was built on land reclaimed from the sea. In fact only about one-tenth of the land was originally here just over a hundred years ago. We have watched this new town being created over the past couple of decades. In fact very few of the original buildings remain.

In 1910 the two principal businesses that existed here were a Bavarian brewery and a macaroni factory. The gas works, originally in the Condamine, came to Fontvieille in the early Twenties. There were also the Electric Power works, two steam laundries and a bakery, two other small works of note, a manufacturer of perfume and an art pottery works.

Even the old stadium, since pulled down, was built in the Thirties on partly reclaimed land. Now the impressive new stadium houses not only a football field, but also swimming and diving pools, a basket-ball indoor arena, squash courts, four floors of parking and many offices. When space is valuable you learn to use every square metre.

Driving around Fontvieille you will be astounded to see a new church, school, fire station, heliport, a permanent circus tent, factories, shops and everything a town's infrastructure needs, even the new port.

The new town has a three star hotel called the ABELLA, where they do excellent three-course lunches at a very reasonable price. But our first call is to another ethnic establishment:

LE MARRAKECH, 32 quai des Sanbarbani

Tel: 93 30 11 41. Fixed price menu: none.

Sadly there is no menu so you need to go with someone who has had some experience of Moroccan food. If there are two of you, I can advise you to try a Briouat Merguez and a Briouat of Kefta as starters, a couscous of chicken and one of lamb as a main course. Their desserts are very sweet, with lots of honey, flaky pastry and nuts. Something very different, but this is super quality and very clean. If you have never eaten Moroccan, this is certainly the place to start.

LE CIRQUE, 16 quai des Sanbarbani

Tel: 92 05 97 99. Closed: Sundays.
Fixed-price menu: none. Brigitte Bille.

Sitting on the terrace viewing the great yachts is certainly part of the fun of this recent addition to Monaco's eating places. Here they offer refined Italian cuisine served in the traditional French way. A good selection of both French and Italian wines.

Last time we visited, there were six of us so it was a fair assessment. We had a variety of starters: *spaghetti all' arabiatta, alla pomodoro, alla putanesca*. The first is hot with chillis, the second is with tomatoes and the last is with anchovies and olives. My wife, of course, chose the risotto with mushrooms. Several had the *sole au trois parfums*; this was three pieces of filleted sole each done in a different flavour. A couple had *steak au poivre* and one had a boring grilled sole. All excellent, served with a selection of vegetables. It always surprises me when you go with a group how often quite a few choose the same dish. You would think they would all be brave and choose differently. The dessert trolley had an imaginative selection so some did have a gamble. With our coffees they brought those lovely Italian macaroon biscuits, the ones wrapped in that fine paper. You can roll the paper into a cylinder and light one end and watch it shoot up to the ceiling.

The meal is verging on expensive yet as it is imaginatively prepared, 250 to 300 francs comes out at the top end of good value.

They also have a small snack restaurant next door called Poisson D'or. Here you can have the *plat du jour* or help yourselves to the hors d'oeuvres for 60 francs. The telephone number for here is 92 05 97 50. Wine is also only 25 francs for the carafe.

ROQUEBRUNE CAP-MARTIN

Roquebrune is an old village perched on the hill side; Cap-Martin is the promontory below. They have now merged into one town, even though each part is very different in character.

To reach the old village go up the D 2564. Surprisingly the village is not perched on the top, like so many here in Provence, but nestles half way up. In fact it was built on a platform created by a landslide in the seventh century. The castle is impressive and dominant, especially when one sees it lit at night. It was established in 970 by the Count of Vintimille, as a fortress on his borders to defend his lands from the invading Saracens.

The old town is a maze of tiny streets and if you are in the region during Easter week they have a marvellous procession. There are a number of restaurants here. If you need an excuse to try one of the following, you can always say that you were going to view the old village. The first you come to on the way up is:

DAME JEANNE, 1 chemin de Sainte Lucie

Tel: 93 35 10 20. Closed: Mondays. Fixed price menu: none. Claude Nobbio.

The ground floor is like a vaulted cellar, great in winter. The first floor has the view so preferable in summer. Madame Nobbio looks after you and takes the orders and does some of the service, assisted by a couple of others.

Their wine list was a mixed bag, a Côtes de Provence Ste Roseline at 125 francs, Côte du Rhône at 80 and 90 francs, their St-Tropez at 85 francs. We chose a Croze Hermitage that wasn't bad at all, in fact had some body. At 90 francs it was one of the cheapest.

I went with a friend from England. He started with cannelloni and I with snails done in a warm sauce with provençal vegetables. He then chose the *magret de canard* and I the *sanglier* (wild boar) with dumplings. Both of us had the *tarte au pomme caramelisée* and coffees.

Our meal was no surprise at just above my limit of 500 francs for two.

Food: 7½   *Ambiance: 8½*   *Service: 7*

LES DEUX FRERES, Place des Deux Frères

Tel: 93 28 99 00. Closed: Thursdays.
Fixed price menu: none. M. In't-Haut.

This building used to be the village school, and the original tiles are still on the floor in the dining room. A Dutch architect bought it and has tastefully renovated it into a small hotel with ten bedrooms and a restaurant. His son, who is the chef, is well qualified having done some of his training with Michel Guerard.

The restaurant is beautifully appointed with a bar, seating for a couple of dozen, and an area in front of the fireplace where one can sit and enjoy coffee after the meal.

The wines are on the pricey side; we chose a Côtes de Provence called Matourne, previously unknown to us, at 87 francs. We were pleasantly surprised.

We started with a duck salad and a *bisque*, both excellent, and these were followed by a *poulet de la ferme* and a *carré d'agneau*. I had chosen the chicken but when the plates were placed before us, I was very tempted by the lamb. 'The grass is always greener on the other side'. My guest upset me by getting quite eloquent on how good it was.

I had been quite good, in fact I was on a diet, no bread, very little wine, etc. My guest should have also been on a diet but ploughed on ordering a *bavarois*. The bill came to 480 francs with everything including service.

Food: 7½   **Ambiance: 8**   **Service: 8**

In summer one can sit outside on the terrace, a superb spot with an excellent view of Monaco.

Onwards and upwards, now we have really entered the old village.

PICCOLO MONDO, 15 rue Grimaldi

Tel: 93 35 19 93. Closed: Mondays.
Fixed price menu: F150. Tony Minetti.

Tony is an Italian who worked on Jersey for over ten years, before he opened his own place here. This is a very small restaurant that seats about twenty-four, with a few more outside on the pavement in summer.

We went for Sunday lunch as he offers a traditional English meal on that day. Usually he has two roasts; one of us had the roast beef, Yorkshire pudding, roast potatoes, gravy and all. The other had the roast pork with plenty of crackling – delicious.

We had starters, avocado with crab and *pâté maison* and the desserts were sherry trifle and apple pie. The wine we chose was an Italian Antinori red. This comes from close to Florence. There were French wines on the list as well. At 100 francs the wine is not given away.

Tony gives you all the trimmings and is very friendly. If you want something different just give him fair warning so he can prepare it for you. Nothing is too much trouble.

Food: 7½   **Ambiance: 7½**   **Service: 7½**

LE GRAND INQUISITEUR, 18 rue du Château

Tel: 93 35 05 37. Closed: Mondays.
Fixed price menus: F130 and F210. Max Valente.

This is the highest placed restaurant in the village, an old stable that is cosy and friendly. The owner cooks and produces some lovely dishes. His wine prices are again on the high side; maybe it is relative to the altitude!

Above Roquebrune on the Grande Corniche is an unbelievable place to build a hotel. Perched and jutting from this high promontory, it looks as if it is ready to fall off:

VISTA PALACE, Grande Corniche

Tel: 93 35 01 50. Closed: lunch in summer.
Fixed price menu: F300. Karl H Vanis.

You may not want to dine here but it is certainly worth a stop, on a clear evening, for a drink in the piano bar. From here you have a spectacular view of the coast from Italy in the East to St -ropez in the West.

From the heights of the Grande Corniche to the sea lapping the rocks at Cap-Martin. The following restaurant is one of our great favourites. On a sunny winter Sunday you will see us leave Monaco, my wife in her trainers and I in my docksiders. Jeans, short-sleeved shirt and a sweater over our shoulders. We walk along the water's edge all the way to Cap-Martin and the:

ROQUE MARTIN, 42 ave Winston Churchill

Tel: 93 35 75 56. Closed: Wednesdays.
Fixed price menu: none. Madame Castro.

This is a lovely restaurant right on the water's edge, with a view to Menton and the Italian Alps. On these sunny winter days we sit on the terrace protected by the glass wind-breakers, lapping up the sun and enjoying our lunch.

We always have *soupe de poisson* or *moules marinières* as starters and a fish grilled or in the oven as our main plate. We seldom have the dessert but always a bottle of wine and some coffee. Pay the bill, usually around the 500 franc mark, then don our sweaters and stroll back. Certainly healthy and most enjoyable.

Food: 7½   *Ambiance:* 8   *Service:* 7½

GORBIO

To reach this medieval fortified village follow the D 23 north-west out of Menton, it is under 10 km. It is neither the most interesting nor the most picturesque of villages but it does have a very good value restaurant:

BEAU SEJOUR, *place du Village*

Tel: 93 41 46 15. Open: lunch all year, dinners June to August. Closed Wednesdays. Fixed price menus: F85 to F145. Yvan Bracco.

Three set menus, F85 and F105 for four courses, six courses at 145 francs. When you arrive you walk into the village bar, and walk the length of the room into another room at right angles to the bar. You notice two things: first the large expanse of windows over-looking a valley; second a small grand piano. Remember the latter as the former is a disappointment.

You are well taken care of by the owner Yvan, and he has one assistant to help him and to look after the bar. The place is casual and friendly. Whilst looking at the menu some radishes and an olive paste dip are placed in front of you. The wine list is small, you won't find any *premier cru* here, but the prices temptingly start at 25/35F for the Cuvée Maison. Even the Côtes de Provence is only 30/50 francs for a half-bottle or bottle.

I dragged my brother, Alex, out of hibernation by offering him a feast that has no equal. He drove and felt the direction I was taking him would lead only to a continually empty stomach. Neither of us was impressed by the village square. However, when we got to our main task we both chose the 85 franc menu and were given as a starter a beautifully presented plate of local specialities, local cured ham, tomatoes, eggs, olives and more. Our main course were *lapin à la marjolaine* and *saumon à l'aneth*; there were two other choices: *daube à la Provençal* or *civet de porcelet*. Our main dishes were wonderfully garnished with *pommes dauphinoises, tomates Provençal* and braised endives. Both of us expressed surprise at the finesse of the dishes; we were expecting more country cooking. A *salade aux noix* followed then cheese or dessert; we both chose the former. Another lovely touch; when we had our coffees we received a small plate of chocolates. All these details make for a so much better meal.

Food; 8   **Ambiance: 7**   *Service: 7½*

The food was much better than the place itself. But I prefer it that way round, though, of course, one would like them equal. But the experience is great value as it cost us only 212 francs. I did not have the heart to tell my brother to pay for this special treat.

Dont forget the piano. If you enjoy jazz you must get there early and tempt Yvan to sit down and play. He is first class.

MONTI

PIERROT-PIERRETTE, place de l'Eglise

Tel: 93 35 79 76. Closed: Mondays.
Fixed price menus: F135 to F200. M. and Mme Mitolo and Son.

Monti is found by following the D 2566 for about 5 km from Menton. The three menus at F135, F165 and 200 francs offer three, four and five courses respectively. The choice for a country place is surprising, including fresh trout, *écrevisse,* home-made ravioli and many more. The family did everything, and were welcoming and friendly. The whole setting had that familiar feeling: clean white table-cloths, beams, comfortable country chairs, and some iron pieces hanging from the walls. I had the 135 franc menu, *truite au bleu* followed by *steak au poivres*. This came with spinach and sautée potatoes. I had three selections from the cheese tray rather than dessert, then a coffee. I accompanied this with a half-bottle of house wine at 34 francs. When the bill arrived at 178 francs I thought, maybe expensive; yet on second thoughts, fresh trout and entrecôte steak, both those items are expensive. All in all not bad value.

Food: 7½   *Ambiance:* 7½   *Service:* 7

MENTON

This particular spot generally has the mildest winters on the Côte d'Azur. The reason for this is it is well protected on all three sides by high mountains, so even the Mistral has no effect. This has meant a large proportion of the winter residents are old and it gave rise to the saying 'Cannes is for living, Monte Carlo is for playing, and Menton is for dying'. Today it is still one of the prettier towns on the Côte and now attitudes are changing and it is beginning to attract younger residents. It still retains its old world, slightly upper class charm.

Menton has had a mixed history, having been a republic in its own right, at various times belonging to France, Italy and Monaco. It is still quiet of an evening in winter, although it does have its winter Festival of lemons and oranges which is worth a visit. Among other points of interest the baroque church of St Michel is worth a visit.

Menton has many restaurants, quite a few open only in summer or at lunch times in winter. It is still a lovely town to just stroll around.

LE MERLE BLANC, 21 rue st Michel

Tel: 93 35 77 53. Closed: Fridays.
Fixed price menus: F78, F90 and F170.

This restaurant in the *zone piéton* is regularly full, as it offers good value. There are three menus, two of three courses at 78F and 90 francs and a four course menu at 170 francs. We have never eaten the largest menu as we find the other two more than adequate, all offering a large choice. The wines as well are within everyone's pocket, the Cuvée des deux Princes at 30/40 francs or the Côte de

Provence AOC at 35/50 francs. A small selection of other wines is also available.

The place is tastefully decorated, stuffed birds and animals being the main decoration. Disappointingly the table-cloths and napkins are of paper, which is not general in France. I last went there with my brother and we both chose the 90 franc menu.

He started with *salade de crudités* and had *lapin* for his main course. I chose the *moules marinières* and the *steak au poivre*. I had the cheese and he the fruit. We enjoyed a bottle of the Cuvée des deux Princes, only a VDQS yet the red was full of body and had quite a nose. With coffees the bill came to around 250 francs. We strolled down the walk-away to where we had left the car, quite content with both meal and price.

Food: 7   *Ambiance: 7*   *Service: 7*

L'OURSIN, 3 rue Trenca

Tel: 93 28 33 62. Closed: Wednesdays.
Fixed price menu: none. M. Casademont.

You don't come here for the decoration, or because it is smart or fashionable. You do come if you want to eat fresh fish. The owner and his staff are all dressed in blue and white striped shirts and light coloured slacks. They look after you professionally yet a little casually, never familiar.

The house white wine is a Domaine de Nestuby, not on your list of those you are intending to lay down, but at 40/60 francs, it is a Blanc de Blanc that is fresh, fruity and easily drinkable. There is a Côtes de Provence at 50/80 francs and others from this price upwards. Such prices are something you have to expect on the front.

We were a party of four and three of us went for the *soupe de poisson* and one had the *palourdes* (clams). We then had a *loup* between two, with coriander and lemon. The other two had *dorade* with onions, tomatoes and tarragon. Both well presented and certainly very succulent and tasty.

The four of us passed up desserts and settled for a couple of espressos each. The bill when it arrived was close to one thousand francs. Yet a good *dorade royal* (pink in colour) in the market is not a cheap item, neither is a *loup de mer.* So if you wish to eat very good fish I think you will find you have to pay for it.

Food: 7½   *Ambiance: 6½*   *Service: 7*

LA TRATTORIA, 123 rue Longue

Tel: 93 28 44 64. Closed: lunches. Fixed price menu: none.
Laurent and Pasquale Fort.

Laurent and Pasquale are brother and sister, both in their early twenties, and they work with their brother-in-law Eric. They come from a restaurant background as their father owns La Marinière on the avenue de la Madone. He did his training in Nice, while she went to the hotelier school in Menton. They open in the evenings and remain open till after all the other restaurants close. In the early hours you find people who work in other establishments finish up here for a snack.

They offer mainly pizzas (30–40 francs), but have a few main dishes (65–80 francs). They are very friendly and relaxed, making this a perfect place for young people who have to bring along their parents as well. The wines are extremely reasonably priced; a *pichet* is 23/32 francs, while a bottle of the local wine is 26/34 francs. A Côtes de Provence is 42/65 francs. They also offer a Beaune and a Côte du Rhône.

When you are seated they bring you toasted bread and a dip. The place has three floors, clean and homely. They have music at weekends, which I am sure is more suitable for youngsters. Two can have a pizza each, plus a *pichet* of wine for about 100 francs. Not bad at all.

Three of us went along and had a bottle of red wine and a *pichet* of rosé, plus two bottles of mineral water. A *steak au poivre* and two veal with a cream sauce, a large dish of mixed vegetables from which you helped yourselves. We had five coffees between us and with these were served a few chocolates, a lovely touch for such an inexpensive restaurant.

The bill for the three of us was 400 francs. The dip and the chocolates are something a great number of other places could learn from these young people.

Food: 7½   *Ambiance: 8*   *Service: 7½*

CHEZ MIREILLE–L'ERMITAGE, 1080 promenade du Soleil

Tel: 93 35 77 23. Closed: Monday dinner and Tuesday.
Fixed price menus: F130 to F220. Jean-Pierre Bisson.

A very traditional restaurant that offers three menus at F130, F165 and F220. For those that want a more formal atmosphere with high standards, this is certainly the best restaurant in Menton. You won't be disappointed.

Food: 8   *Ambiance: 7*   *Service: 7½*

VEGETARIAN FOOD

During the past few years the number of vegetarian restaurants has grown. Many of the well known places serve some vegetarian food. One of the leading vegetarian cooks is Jean Montagard, who teaches at the hotelier schools in Nice and Menton. He has published a guide and recipe books on his speciality.

I list below, in alphabetical town order, some of the restaurants that I know serve vegetarian meals. All these are in the Alpes Maritimes.

Cagnes–sur–Mer	LA COMEDIE	Tel: 93 73 44 64
	GRAIN SAUVAGE	Tel: 93 73 10 00
La Gaude	LE CIGALON	Tel: 93 24 47 77
Menton	LA SOURCE VITALE	Tel: 93 28 23 88
Monaco	LOUIS XV	Tel: 93 30 23 11
Nice	TOSELLO	Tel: 93 62 10 20
St Laurent	YAN TSEU KIANG	Tel: 93 31 92 82
Vence	CHATEAU DES AROMES	Tel: 93 58 70 24
	REUNION DE FAMILLE	Tel: 93 24 18 37

ALPHABETICAL LIST OF RESTAURANTS

If one multiplies the PRICE number by 100 it should give the maximum cost of one person's meal in Francs.

Page	Restaurant	Town	Food	Ambience	Service	Price
131	L'Amandier de Mougins	Mougins	8	8½	8	2½
113	Amiral	Ste Maxime	8	7	7½	3
31	L'Amourie	St Romain Viennois	8	7½	7 ½	1½
133	L'Amphitryon	Grasse	7½	7½	7½	2½
172	L 'A Propos	Nice	7½	7	7	2
56	Auberge Cavalière	Les-Saintes-Maries	8	8	7½	2½
42	Auberge de la Loube	Buoux	7	8	8	2
182	Auberge de la Madone	Peillon	7½	7½	7	3
102	Auberge de la Mole	La Mole	8	8½	8	2½
157	Auberge des Seigneurs	Vence	8	9	7½	2½
135	Auberge du Chantegrill	Peymeinade	7	7	7	2
46	Auberge du Cheval Blanc	La Bastide des Jourdans	7	7	7	1½
147	Auberge du Jarrier	Biot	8	8	7½	4½
156	Auberge du Port	Cagnes-sur-Mer	7	7	7	2½
95	Auberge du Puits Jaubert	Montauroux	7½	8½	7½	2½
139	Auberge Fleurie	Valbonne	8	7½	7½	2½
86	Auberge Josse	Lorgues	7	7	7	1½
93	Auberge la Becassière	Montauroux	8	7½	7½	2½
75	Auberge le Vieux Pressoir	Brignoles	7	7	7½	1½
92	Auberge Mestre Cornille	Seillans	7	7½	7	2½
179	Auberge Pierres Longues	Nice-la Trinité	7	7	7	2½
92	Auberge Pierrot	Bargemon	7½	7½	7½	3½
142	Auberge St Donat	Plascassier	7	7½	7½	1
121	Au Mal Assis	Cannes	8	7½	8	3

Page	Restaurant	Town	Food	Ambience	Service	Price
175	Aux Gourmets	Nice	8	7½	7	3
167	Barale	Nice	7½	8	7	2½
112	Le Baron	St Tropez	8½	8	8½	5
160	La Baronnie	St Paul de Vence	8	8	8	5½
212	Beau Séjour	Gorbio	7	7	7½	1½
190	Beleze	Eze	6½	6½	6	1½
126	La Belle Otero	Cannes	8½	8½	8½	8
149	Belles Rives	Juan-les-Pins	8	8	8	5½
189	La Bergerie	Eze	7½	7½	7½	3
51	Le Bistro du Paradou	Le Paradou	7	8	7½	1½
44	Le Bistrot	Lourmarin	7	7	7	1½
132	Le Bistrot de Mougins	Mougins	8	8	7½	2½
142	Le Bistrot de Valbonne	Valbonne	8	8	7	3½
171	Le Bistrot du Florian	Nice	8	8	8	2½
61	Le Bistrot Latin	Aix-en-Provence	8	8	7½	2½
151	La Bonne Auberge	Antibes	9½	8½	9	6½
71	La Bonne Etape	Chateau-Arnoux	9	8½	8½	7
105	La Bretonnière	Grimaud	9	8½	9	4
63	La Brocherie	Aix-en-Provence	7	7½	7	1½
119	La Brocherie	La Napoule	7½	8½	6½	4½
159	La Brouette	Vence	7½	8	7	2½
56	Le Bruleur de Loups	Les-Saintes-Maries	7	7½	7	2½
37	Brunel	Avignon	8½	7½	7½	4½
50	La Cabro d'Or	Baux-de-Provence	8½	8	8	5½
108	Café de France	Grimaud	7	7	7½	2½
146	Café de la Poste	Biot	8	8	6½	3
202	Café de Paris	Monte-Carlo	7½	8½	7½	3½
38	Café des Artistes	Avignon	7½	8	8	2½
48	Café des Arts	St Rémy-de-Provence	7½	8	7	1½
58	Café des Arts	Salon-de-Provence	7	7	7	1
168	Café de Turin	Nice	8½	8½	7	2
155	Le Cagnard	Cagnes Haut	8½	9	8	6½
168	La Cambuse	Nice	7	7	7	2
123	La Cannasuisse	Cannes	7	7	7	2½
190	Du Cap Roux	Eze-sur-Mer	7½	7	7	2
184	Carpaccio	Villefranche	7½	8	7½	3

Alphabetical List of Restaurants

Page	Restaurant	Town	Food	Ambience	Service	Price
112	Chabichou	St Tropez	8½	8	8½	6
176	Le Chamois	St-Martin-Vesubie	7½	7	7½	2
171	Chantecler	Nice	9½	9½	9½	6½
167	Chapon Fin	Nice	7½	7	7½	2½
158	Château des Aromes	Vence	8	8½	7½	4½
188	Château Eza	Eze Village	8½	8½	7	5
158	Château St Martin	Vence	8½	9	8½	6
45	La Chaumière	Lauris	7½	8	7	3
177	La Chaumière	Nice-Eze	9	8½	7½	4
188	Chèvre d'Or	Eze Village	8	8	7½	6
69	Chez Gilbert	Cassis	7½	8	7½	1½
67	Chez Madie	Marseille	8	8½	7	2
191	Chez Michel	Cap d'Ail	7	7	7	2
169	Chez Michel	Nice	8½	7½	7½	3½
217	Chez Mireille-l'Ermitage	Menton	8	7	7½	3
75	Chez Nous	St Maximin	8	7½	7	3
37	Christian Etienne	Avignon	8	7	7	3
167	Cicion-Mallen	Nice	7	7	7	2
207	Le Cirque	Fontvieille	7½	8½	7	4
63	La Clemence	Aix-en-Provence	6½	6½	7	1
64	Le Clos de la Violette	Aix-en-Provence	8	7½	8	5
160	La Colombe d'Or	St Paul de Vence	7½	8½	7	4
102	La Corniche	Toulon	8½	7½	8	4
126	La Côte	Cannes	8½	8½	8½	7
54	La Côte d'Adam	Arles	7	7	7	1½
203	La Coupole	Monte-Carlo	8½	7½	8	5
68	Cousin Cousine	Marseille	7½	7	7½	2½
208	Dame Jeanne	Roquebrune	7½	8½	7	3½
113	Le Daniele	Ste Maxime	7½	7½	7	2½
102	Le Dauphin	Toulon	8	6½	7½	2½
170	Les Dents de la Mer	Nice	7½	8½	8	3½
209	Les Deux Frères	Roquebrune	7½	8	8	3½
199	Dolce Vita	Monte-Carlo	7	6½	7	1½
37	Les Domaines	Avignon	8	7½	7½	2½
166	Don Camillo	Nice	8½	7½	7½	5

Page	Restaurant	Town	Food	Ambience	Service	Price
189	Eze Country Club	Eze	8	7½	7½	4½
158	La Farigoule	Vence	7½	7	7	2½
131	Ferme de Mougins	Mougins	8½	8	8	5
128	Feu Follet	Mougins	8½	8½	8½	2½
58	Le Fin Bec	Orgon	7	6½	6½	1
173	Flo-Nice	Nice	8	7½	7	2½
175	Le Floride	Nice	7	7	7	1
87	Le Four	Lorgues	6	6½	7	1½
93	France	Fayence	7½	8	7	2½
120	Frederic	Ile St Honorat	8	8	7	5
64	Les Frères Lani	Aix-en-Provence	8½	7	7½	4
201	Fuji	Monte-Carlo	9	8	7½	5
111	Le Girelier	St Tropez	7½	7½	7½	3
127	La Gousse d'Ail	Vallauris	8	7½	7½	3
53	Grand Café de la Bourse	Arles	7	6½	7	2
174	Grand Café des Arts	Nice	7½	8	7½	1½
84	Grand Hôtel Allègre	Salernes	7½	8	7	1½
210	Le Grand Inquisiteur	Roquebrune Cap-Martin	7	7	7	1½
72	Le Grand Paris	Digne	7½	8	7	5
205	Le Gratin	Monte-Carlo	8½	8	8	4
185	La Grignotière	Villefranche	8	8	8	2
80	Grillade au Feu de Bois	Le Luc-Flassans	7½	7½	7½	2½
59	Grill de Provence	Lancon	7½	6½	7	1½
203	Grill Hôtel de Paris	Monte-Carlo	8½	8	8½	6
37	Hiely-Lucullus	Avignon	8½	7½	7½	4½
57	Hostellerie du Pont du Gau	Les-Saintes-Maries	7	7½	7½	2
161	Issautier	St Martin du Var	9	8½	8½	6
124	Le Jardin	Cannes	7½	7½	7½	1½
99	Le Lingousto	Cuers	9	8	8½	4½
168	Lou Balico	Nice	7	7	7	2
114	Lou Calen	Fréjus	8½	8	8½	2½
54	Lou Caleu	Arles	8	7½	7	2½
88	Lou Cigaloun	St Antonin du Var	8	7½	7½	3
90	Lou Galoubet	Draguignan	8	7	8	2
54	Lou Marques	Arles	8	8½	8	5

Alphabetical List of Restaurants

Page	Restaurant	Town	Food	Ambience	Service	Price
130	Mas Candille	Mougins	8	8½	8	3½
51	Mas d'Aigret	Baux-de-Provence	8	8½	8	5
161	Mas d'Artigny	St Paul de Vence	8	8	8	6
112	Mas de Chastelas	St Tropez	8½	8½	8	5
35	Mas de Cure Bourse	L'Isle sur la Sorgue	8	7½	7½	2
77	Mas de la Cascade	Brignoles	8	8	8	2½
186	Le Massoury	Villefranche	8	8½	7	5
150	Matin	Antibes	7	7	7	2
167	Meranda	Nice	7½	8	7	2
214	Le Merle Blanc	Menton	7	7	7	1½
122	Le Mesclun	Cannes	8	8	7½	4
67	Miramar	Marseille	8½	8	8	5
44	Moulin de Lourmarin	Lourmarin	8	8½	8½	3½
131	Moulin de Mougins	Mougins	9	9	9	8
142	Moulin des Moines	Valbonne	7½	7½	7½	3
131	Les Muscadins	Mougins	8	8	8	4½
180	Napoleon	La Turbie	7½	6	7½	2
175	La Nissarda	Nice	7	7	6½	1½
32	L'Orangerie	Carpentras	7½	7½	7	2½
215	L'Oursin	Menton	7½	6½	7	3½
67	L'Oursinade	Marseille	8½	7	8	4
82	L'Oustalet	Le Canet des Maures	7½	7	7½	2
49	Oustau de Baumanière	Baux de Provence	9	9	8½	8
126	La Palme d'Or	Cannes	8½	8½	8½	8
30	Le Parvis	Orange	7½	7½	7½	2½
155	Des Peintres	Cagnes Haut	7½	8½	7	3
198	Le Périgordin	Monte-Carlo	8	8½	7½	2½
73	Ma Petite Auberge	Digne	6½	7½	6½	1½
66	Le Petit Nice	Marseille	8½	9	8½	7½
133	Le Petit Prince	Cabris	8	8	8	2½
73	Le Petit St Jean	Digne	6½	6½	7	2
97	Le Petit Vatel	Callian	8	7½	7	3
154	Le Picadero	Cagnes-sur-Mer	9	8	8	3
210	Piccolo Mondo	Roquebrune	7½	7½	7½	3
213	Pierrot-Pierrette	Monti	7½	7½	7	2

Eating Out in Provence

Page	Restaurant	Town	Food	Ambience	Service	Price
204	Polpetta	Monte-Carlo	7½	8½	7	3
147	La Pousse-Pousse	Juan-les-Pins	7½	8	7½	3
41	Prévot	Cavaillon	9	8	8	4
205	Pulcinella	Monte-Carlo	7	7½	7	2
125	Le Ragtime	Cannes	7½	9	7½	4
174	Le Raja	Nice	8	8	8	2½
199	La Rascasse	Monte-Carlo	7½	7½	7½	2½
34	La Rascasse d'Argent	Isle-sur-la-Sorgue	7½	6	7½	1½
173	Le Régency	Nice	8½	8	8	4
131	Relais à Mougins	Mougins	8	8	8	5
181	Relais Chez Cotton	Peille	8	8	8	2
138	Relais de la Vignette	Valbonne	8	8	7½	3
143	Relais de Sartoux	Plascassier	7½	8	7½	3
192	Le Restaurant	Beausoleil	8½	8	7½	3
153	Restaurant de Bacon	Cap d'Antibes	8½	8½	8	6½
50	La Riboto de Taven	Les Baux-de-Provence	7½	8	7½	4
150	Le Romarin	Antibes	7½	7½	7½	1½
211	Roque Martin	Cap-Martin	7½	8	7½	3½
126	Royal Gray	Cannes	9	9	9	8½
167	Le Safari	Nice	7	7	7	2
200	Saint-Benoît	Monte-Carlo	8	8	7½	4
185	Saint-Pierre	Villefranche	8½	7	7	3½
203	Salle Belle Epoque	Monte-Carlo	8	9½	8	5
204	Sans Souci	Monte-Carlo	8	7½	7½	3
105	Les Santons	Grimaud	8½	8	8½	6
162	Les Santons	Levens	8	6½	7½	2
33	Le Saule Pleureur	Carpentras	8	8	7½	4
110	Sénequier	St Tropez	8	8	8	1½
187	Le Sloop	Cap-Ferrat	8½	7½	8	4
109	La Speghetta	Grimaud	7	7	7½	1½
147	Les Terraillers	Biot	8	8½	8	4½
149	La Terrasse	Juan-les-Pins	9	8½	9	6
141	La Terrasse	Valbonne	7½	7	7½	1½
172	La Toque Blanche	Nice	8½	8	8	2½
58	La Touloubre	Salon-de-Provence	7½	7½	7	2
216	La Trattoria	Menton	7½	8	7½	2